TEHUANTEPEC

THE

TEHUANTEPEC RAILWAY

ITS LOCATION

FEATURES AND ADVANTAGES

UNDER THE LA SERE GRANT OF

1869

D. APPLETON & CO
90, 92 AND 94 GRAND STREET, NEW YORK
1869

BAKER & GODWIN, PRINTERS,
Printing House Square, N. Y.

THERE

ARE FEW MEN LIVING

TO WHOM AMERICAN COMMERCIAL

DEVELOPMENT IS MORE LARGELY INDEBTED THAN TO

Marshall O. Roberts.

IN THE TRUE SPIRIT OF AN EMINENT MERCHANT, HE HAS DEVOTED YEARS OF PATIENT ENERGY AND OF LIBERAL AND FAR-SEEING ENTERPRISE TO THE GRAND WORK OF OPENING AND KEEPING OPEN THE INTER-OCEANIC GATEWAYS OF THE WESTERN CONTINENT, AND PROVIDING NEW CHANNELS FOR THE COMMERCE OF THE ORIENT. IT IS BELIEVED THAT HE IS NOW ABOUT TO REALIZE ANOTHER OF THOSE SAGACIOUS PROPHECIES OF THE ROUTES OF COMMERCE WHICH HAVE WON HIM HIS PRESENT PROUD POSITION AMONG THE MERCANTILE LEADERS OF THE NEW WORLD. TO HIM THIS MODEST VOLUME, DEVOTED TO THE DEFENCE AND ELUCIDATION OF IDEAS WHICH ARE DEAR TO HIS HEART AND HOPES, AS

THE LEADING PROMOTER OF THE

TEHUANTEPEC RAILWAY,

IS

INSCRIBED.

CONTENTS.

PART I.

PART II.

ILLUSTRATIONS.

PART I.

PART II.

2

ERRATA.

Part II, page 13, line 23; for CUBA, read JAPAN.

" " 69, in title of illustration; read PIEDRA LAGARTO.

INTRODUCTION.

THE TEHUANTEPEC RAILWAY COMPANY invites attention to a Grant or Concession for seventy years, including large grants of land, made by the Government of Mexico, on the 6th of October, 1867, to a Company to be formed by Don Emilio La-Sere, to open interoceanic communication across the Isthmus of Tehuantepec, by railroad, carriage-road, and telegraph line. It is free from all taxation or imposts of any kind by the Government, except the payment of eight per cent. of the net profits of the enterprise, whenever dividends shall be declared for the stockholders, and twelve cents for each through passenger. This grant was modified and confirmed by the Congress of that Republic on the 29th of December, 1868; approved by the President, January 2d, 1869; and published in the Official Gazette of that Government on the 4th of January, 1869.

Pursuant to said grant, Don Emilio La-Sere formed the "Tehuantepec Railway Company," composed wholly of citizens of the United States. This Company, in November, 1868, procured from the General Assembly of the

State of Vermont* an act establishing its incorporation, with a capital of eighteen millions of dollars ($18,000,000), divided into shares of $100 each; and received from said La-Sere an assignment of the grant or concession. On the 2d day of March, 1869, to comply with the 16th article of the grant, the Company gave to the Republic of Mexico its bond in $100,000, which was accepted and approved as satisfactory by Sr. Don Juan N. Navarro, Consul-General of Mexico in the United States, on April 14, 1869, under instructions from his Government.

On the 20th of April the Consul-General notified the Company that the President of Mexico had, on the 28th of March, appointed the directors to which it is entitled under the 30th article of the grant.

Col. Julius W. Adams, Consulting Engineer of the Company, eminent in his profession, prepared in August, 1868, and the Company adopted, a general project for the construction of the proposed works, also a map of the Isthmus of Tehuantepec, showing the proposed lines of railway, carriage-road and telegraph, which were submitted to the Mexican Government, January 5th, 1869, and were approved.

The form of the mortgage, and of the bonds which the Company is authorized to issue in aid of the construction, repair, and maintenance of the works, were prepared by learned counsel, and were adopted by the Company,

---

* The 16th article of the Grant, provides that the Company shall be organized according to the laws of *one* of the States of the American Union. The Legislature of Vermont was the only one in session at that time.

and submitted for and received the approval of the Government, January 5th, 1869. Official documents and further details will be found in the body of this work.

It admits of but little doubt that the discoveries of Columbus arose less from a conviction in his own mind that a new continent would reward his exertions, than from a far-sighted conclusion to which he had arrived, that the true connection of old Spain with the Indies lay in the western direction rather than in the east. The whole of the discoveries at the time of his death embraced the various islands of the West Indies and the coast of Honduras, and he died in the belief that he had accomplished the object of his earliest efforts.

Explorations under others extended to the coasts of Florida on the north and Darien on the south; but the Mexican Gulf, sweeping far into the interior, with its concealed riches, remained as yet unexplored. What he aimed to accomplish—a ready passage to the east by traveling westward—is left for American enterprise.

Diego, the son and successor of Columbus, first colonized Cuba, or Fernandina, as it was called, and Velasquez, the governor of that island, pushed his explorations from St. Jago, his capital, around the coast of Yucatan, and in 1519 organized the expedition under Hernando Cortez, which, landing at Vera Cruz, resulted in the conquest of Mexico. The first care of Cortez was to secure his conquest. The harbor of Vera Cruz being considered as dangerous, even for the small vessels then in use, he sent "a commission composed of his pilots and others," who surveyed the coast south of Vera Cruz for a distance of sixty leagues, as far as the great river Goatzacoalcos, which seemed to offer the best, indeed, the only accommodation, for a safe and suitable harbor. A spot was selected at its mouth for a fortified post, and a colony under Velasquez de Leon was established there in 1519.

Subsequently, in 1520, an addition was made to the colony, under Diego de Ordaz.

It appears in the celebrated letter of Cortez to the Emperor Charles V., to have been an object of intense interest with him to discover some strait which might naturally unite the two seas, but, as his hopes declined in this respect, he conceived the idea of a lucrative speculation by means of a carriage road over the Isthmus of Tehuantepec, to supply Spain with the spices of the East Indies and the products of such new regions as he expected to discover; and Humboldt remarks in reference to the road, that the River Goatzacoalcos furnished great facilities for transporting across the Isthmus from Vera Cruz materials to build vessels which he fitted out in Tehuantepec for the Pacific; and as an evidence of the views which Cortez entertained of this part of the country, he selected large tracts of land on the Goatzacoalcos River, and in Oaxaca, in the neighborhood of Tehuantepec. These estates were confirmed to him by the Emperor Charles V., and were cultivated and the mines worked by Cortez to great profit, and his descendants to this day possess large tracts of land in this neighborhood known as the estates of the "Marquesanas;" and during the lifetime of the conqueror he never lost sight of the advantages to be realized by establishing and maintaining the transit of the Isthmus by this most favorable route. On the death of Cortez no one appeared on the stage to take an interest in the project, and the government of Spain, occupied in conquests elsewhere, allowed the subject to sink into comparative oblivion.

Towards the close of the seventeenth century, Dampier made an exploration of the country, and speaks of the "bar of Goatzacoalaz as less dangerous than any on the coast, with two fathoms of water, and but little sea."

In 1745, the project of opening the Tehuantepec route was again revived, and the viceroy of Mexico was urged to make the Goatzacoalcos a port of entry; but merchants interested in other parts of the country, particularly at Vera Cruz and Acapulco, made such representations at the court of Madrid that an order was obtained prohibiting, under the penalties of regal displeasure, any revival of the subject. But in 1774, Don Antonio M. Bucareli, viceroy of Mexico, ordered Don Augustin Cramer, governor of the San Juan de Ulloa, an engineer by profession, to make a survey of the whole route. He confirms the previous statement of the depth of water on the bar at the mouth of the river, and adds that the bar is a permanent one, never having changed in depth of water since its discovery. His survey was made for the purpose of opening water communication between the two oceans, the entire practicability of which he demonstrates, and at a comparatively small cost, and he remarks on the facilities which exist for a good road to Tehuantepec. These results, as also those to the same purport furnished at a later day by the viceroys of Mexico, Revillagigedo and Iturrigaray, the importance of which was urged upon the Spanish Cortes, failed to elicit any response or action from the government of Spain, which was fast losing its hitherto well earned character for energy and enterprise. However, in 1814, the Spanish Cortes waked up sufficiently to issue a decree for the opening of the canal by way of the Isthmus of Tehuantepec, in preference to that of Nicaragua or Panama; but the political distractions which shortly followed, and the subsequent independence of Mexico, left the government of Spain without either the means or the power to promote such a scheme.

In 1820, William D. Robinson, an American citizen, who had spent considerable time on the Isthmus, published the results of his observations on the various interoceanic routes, and drew the attention of commercial men to the advantages of this route. He says, speaking of the Goatzacoalcos, that "it is the only port in the Mexican Gulf where vessels of war or others of a large size can enter, and it is far superior to Pensacola or Espiritu Santo."

When the Mexicans had established their independence, their first natural desire was to develop the elements of prosperity which their territory possessed. In 1824, the State of Vera

Cruz and the Federal Government appointed each a commission to survey the Isthmus, consisting of Don J. de Ortiz and Col. Juan de Orbegozo; but from the engrossing political contests in the State, the government was for some years prevented from attempting the realization of this grand enterprise, and it was not until 1842 that, upon the representation of Don José de Garay, the Government of Santa Anna conferred upon him an exclusive grant with liberal provisions, to construct and operate a line of railroads in connection with river navigation, to be operated by steam power from ocean to to ocean across the Isthmus of Tehuantepec.

So important and valuable was this transit considered by the Government of the United States, in 1847, the time the treaty of peace with the Republic of Mexico engaged the attention of the Administration of Mr. Polk, that the following correspondence took place:

MR. BUCHANAN, SECRETARY OF STATE,

TO

MR. TRIST, UNITED STATES COMMISSIONER TO MEXICO.

Extract.

DEPARTMENT OF STATE,
WASHINGTON, April 15th, 1847.

* * * *

1. " Instead of Fifteen Millions of dollars stipulated to be " paid by the fifth articles, for the extension of our boundary " over New Mexico, and Upper and Lower California, you " may increase the amount to any sum not exceeding thirty " millions of dollars, payable by instalments of three mil- " lions per annum, provided the right of passage and transit " across the *Isthmus of Tehuantepec*, secured to the United " States by the 8th article of the *Projét* shall form a part of " the treaty."—*Executive Doc. No.* 69, 1*st Sess.*, 30*th Congress.*

Instructions of the Mexican Government to their Commissioners, 29th August, 1847.

Extract.

*   *   *   *

" As regards the privilege solicited by the Government " of the United States to navigate the river Tehuantepec, or " to traffic upon any way or road that may be established " between the two seas, the Government of Mexico absolutely " denies or refuses to concede any such right."—*Senate Doc. No.* 52, 1*st Sess.*, 30*th Cong., vol.* 7, *page* 332.

This offer (sufficient nearly to build two such railroads as this Company propose to construct), it must be remembered, was made *before* the acquisition of California; and, although we now have the Union Pacific Railroad built, history will demonstrate in twenty-five years that the new impetus given to the settlement of the Pacific coast, and the trade with the Indies, will require these, and several more railways, to supply the commerce of the world.

It is but just to the government of Mexico, to state here, that her refusal to entertain the proposition made on the part of the government of the United States, was wholly based on the ground that it had already given to Don José de Garay a concession embracing the entire question. Notwithstanding the refusal of Mexico, at that time, to cede to the United States the right of transit, the grant to Garay having been subsequently annulled, and a new grant to citizens of the United States having been made by Mexico, the protection of the latter was embraced in the eighth article of the treaty concluded between the Republic of Mexico and the United States of America, dated at the City of Mexico on the 30th of

December, 1853, and amended and exchanged at the City of Washington on the 30th of June, 1854, known as "The Gadsden Treaty."

Garay, though himself a gentleman of enterprise and energy, failed to enlist the proper material for the completion of his scheme, and the grant to him was revoked. Since that date, under the various governments of Mexico, there have been three grants issued to various parties for the accomplishment of this project, all of of which for various reasons have failed and been annulled by the Government itself. The grant to La Sere is the only one in existence, and is owned by the Tehuantepec Railway Company, which has settled all out-standing claims relative to this Isthmian transit, whether in law or equity, and now enjoys its title in peace.

It is impossible to overestimate the advantages, both immediate and prospective, which must result to the United States and to Mexico, as well as to the commerce of the world, from the establishment of a rapid and safe inter-oceanic communication across the Isthmus of Tehuantepec, the gateway between the Gulf and the Pacific Ocean.

The neighboring regions of Central America, which are now compelled to seek an outlet elsewhere for their valuable productions, would, in the event of the opening of this route, be drawn by the most powerful of all ties, the tie of a direct and visible commercial interest, into most desirable relations with the United States; while the splendid Mexican provinces on both coasts, which are by no means fully developed by reason of their want of easy access to the markets of the world, would be enlivened by immigration, and enriched by the commercial development of their mineral and vegetable wealth.

At the present day, lines of steamships, American, English, and French, in connection with a railway across the Isthmus of Panama, are maintained and made immensely profitable by the commerce which unites the wealthy and increasing population of the Pacific coast of North and South America with the United States and with Europe. Yet the commerce thus carried on is forced to make a long and circuitous journey, involving unnecessary expenditure both of time and money, and yearly exposing thousands of passengers of all nations to the unwholesome influences of the climate of the Isthmus of Panama.*

No one, therefore, can doubt that a line of communication across the Isthmus of Tehuantepec, passing through a region the superior healthiness of which has been attested by repeated surveys, and shortening the distance about 1,500 miles, *statute*, and time of transit between New York and San Francisco no less than six or seven days, must speedily draw to itself

---

* Don Alonzo Guzman, in the account of his voyage from the island of Española to Peru, via Panama, in 1534, published by the Hakluyt Society, in 1862, says, that on his arrival at the port of Nombre de Dios, in the Province of Castilla del Oro, he learned that the native name of the place means *Bones*, and was so called on account of the number of people who have died there.

the greater portion of the great interoceanic trade, and become, in fact, the highway from Europe and Atlantic America to the States of the Pacific, to South America, to the islands of the Southern Sea, and the older continents of Asia and of Africa.

In a political point of view it plainly matters but little by whom this great work shall be constructed, if only it be under the control and supervision of the Mexican Government.

We have seen in the old world that the independence of Egypt, which it was first supposed would be threatened by the construction of the Suez Canal by English and French enterprise across Egyptian territory, to unite the Mediterranean Sea with the Indian Ocean, has in fact been fortified thereby, and made more important to all civilized nations.

A similar effect must assuredly follow in Mexico, from similar causes, the more especially that in a few years the increase of wealth and population accruing to Mexico from an interoceanic route and the settlement of the lands of the Company, must render the Republic, already so populous and so rich, stronger than ever before to protect its own interests and maintain its own dignity.

As the public are but little apprised of the peculiar features, geographical, physical, or commercial, of the several Isthmian interoceanic transits, the aim of the present paper is to sketch, as briefly as possible, the advantages to be anticipated by adopting the route by way of the Isthmus of Tehuantepec. The exposition of the Isthmian routes in detail is foreign to our object, although a most careful comparative ex amination has been made of them all, as well as of the trans-continental routes between the Atlantic and Pacific Oceans. The conclusions that have been arrived at, are based upon data derived from the best known sources, official and private; and, while we disparage no other transit, we present to the public the best and most reliable array of facts to show the superiority of the Isthmus of Tehuantepec, especially so far as the United States is concerned.

We would wish to acknowledge in this place our indebtedness to the individual sources from which we have drawn our information, but they are so extended that we can only refer in general to the list of authorities published in the report of Rear Admiral Davis, U. S. N., superintendent of the National Observatory, in relation to the various proposed lines for interoceanic canals and railroads between the Atlantic and Pacific Oceans, communicated to Congress, July, 1866. Most of the papers referred to in this list bearing upon the route in question have been open to us, and in addition we have had the advantage of personal intercourse with gentlemen resident on the Isthmus, or who have visited it either for commercial purposes or scientific exploration. We must, however, make one exception in the list of authorities quoted by Admiral Davis, and particularize as a source from which we have largely drawn, the admirable report of J. J. Williams, C. E., New York, 1852, being the result of a survey for a railroad to connect the Atlantic and Pacific Oceans, made by the scientific commission under the direction of Major (now Major General) J. G. Barnard, U. S. Engineers.

In conclusion we may say of the vignette on the title page, that it illustrates the twenty-second article of the grant, the determination of the Mexican Government, the wishes of the Company, and the hopes of Commerce.

SIMON STEVENS,

PRESIDENT

Tehuantepec Railroad Company.

174 CHAMBERS STREET, NEW YORK.
June 17*th*, 1869.

TEHUANTEPEC CONCESION DE LA SERE.

Mexico, *Lúnes, 4 de Enero de* 1869.

Ministerio de Fomento, Colonizacion, Industria y Comercio.

El C. presidente de la república se ha servido dirigirme el decreto que sigue:

"*BENITO JUAREZ, Presidente constitucional de los Estados-Unidos mexicanos, á todos sus habitantes, sabed;*

"Que el Congreso de la Union ha decretado lo siguiente:

"El congreso de la Union decreta:

"Art. 1.—El decreto expedido por el Ejecutivo en 6 de Octubre de 1867, autorizando á D. Emilio La-Sere, ó á la compañía que él formara para abrir la comunicacion interoceánica por el Istmo de Tehuantepec, queda modificado en los términos siguientes:

"Art. 2.—Se autoriza á la compañía que forme D. Emilio La-Sere, para la apertura de la comunicacion interoceánica por el Istmo de Tehuantepec, con las condiciones expresadas en este decreto.

"Art. 3.—La compañía que forme La-Sere, podrá hacer la comunicacion por agua, en la parte navegable del rio Goatzacoalcos; y en donde ella concluya principiarán los caminos á que se refiere el artículo siguiente; pero si no juzga conveniente hacer uso del rio, comenzarán los caminos desde el punto de su desembocadura.

TEHUANTEPEC LA SÈRE GRANT.

MEXICO, *Monday, 4th January*, 1869.

Department of Improvement, Colonization, Industry, and Commerce.

The Citizen President of the Republic has been pleased to address me the following decree:

BENITO JUAREZ, Constitutional President of the Mexican United States, to all its inhabitants:

Be it known that the Congress of the Union has decreed the following:

The Congress of the Union decrees:

ARTICLE 1ST.—The decree issued by the Executive on the 6th October, 1867, authorizing Don Emilio La Sère, or the company that he may form, to open the inter-oceanic communication across the Isthmus of Tehuantepec, is modified in the following terms: Decree of 1867 to be modified.

ARTICLE 2D.—Authorization is granted to the company, that Don Emilio La Sère may form, to open the inter-oceanic communication across the Isthmus of Tehuantepec, with the conditions expressed in this decree. Authority to open communication across Isthmus.

ARTICLE 3D.—The company to be formed by La Sère may establish communication by water in the navigable portion of the Goatzacoalcos River, and, where that ends, the roads will commence as referred to in the following articles; but if it should not be deemed expedient to use the river, the roads will commence at the mouth of the same. By roads or by water and roads.

"Art. 4.—La compañía La-Sère deberá construir un ferrocarril de la mejor clase, que partiendo del punto en que termine la navegacion del rio Goatzacoalcos ó de su desembocadura, segun lo expresa el artículo anterior, llegue hasta el puerto de la Ventosa, ó cualquiera otro del Pacífico que se creyere mas conveniente que este. Entretanto se concluye el camino de fierro, La-Sère establecerá la comunicacion por medio de un camino carretero, que conservará en buen estado de servicio, y con los puentes necesarios para el tránsito de carruages que conduzcan pasageros y mercancías de poco peso.

"Art. 5.—Hechos los reconocimientos necesarios para el ferrocarril y para el camino carretero, y levantados los planos correspondientes por los ingenieros, se someterán á la aprobacion del Gobierno general, sin lo cual no podrán ponerse en ejecucion.

"Art. 6.—La compañía La-Sère avisará oportunamente al Gobierno cuándo debe empezar el reconocimiento del terreno por donde han de pasar los caminos, para que aquel nombre el comisionado ó comisionados que lo representen en las operaciones que hayan de practicarse, pagándose por la compañía los honorarios de aquellos. Para el deslinde de los terrenos baldíos que deban cederse á la compañía, intervendrán los peritos que nombre el Gobierno, pagándose tambien sus honorarios por ella.

"Art. 7.—En el término de diez y ocho meses, contados desde la fecha de esta concesion, deberán estar hechas las exploraciones del terreno, levantados y presentados los planos que marquen la direccion de los caminos, y sometidos á la aprobacion del Gobierno, al que se dará aviso dentro de los primeros seis meses, de que va á procederse á los trabajos, á fin de que el comisionado ó comisionados de que habla la primera parte del artículo anterior, se hallen presentes para inspeccionar las obras que se ejecuten.

Article 4th.—The La Sère Company is bound to construct a first-class railroad, starting from the point where navigation on the Goatzacoalcos River terminates, or from its mouth in conformity with the preceding article, and continue said road to the port of Ventosa, or to any other port on the Pacific that may be deemed more suitable. While the railroad is being finished, La Sère will establish the communication by means of a carriage road, which he will keep in a good serviceable condition, and with bridges necessary for the passage of vehicles carrying passengers and merchandise of light burden.

Railroad to Pacific. Carriage-road meanwhile.

Article 5th.—The necessary surveys being made for the railroad and for the carriage road, and the corresponding maps or plans being made by the engineers, these will be submitted for the approbation of the General Government, without which they will not be allowed to be carried into execution.

Surveys and maps to be approved by Government.

Article 6th.—The La Sère Company shall notify the Government opportunely of the time when the survey of the lands through which the roads are to pass, is to begin, so that the Government may appoint the commissioner or commissioners who are to represent it in the operations which will follow, their fees to be paid by the company. For the demarcation of the unclaimed lands to be ceded to the company, the experts that the Government may name will intervene; these also will be paid by the company.

Before survey, Government to appoint commissioners.

Article 7th.—Within the term of eighteen months, counting from the date of this grant, the surveys of the ground are to be made, the plans showing the lines of the roads are to be made, and submitted for the approbation of the Government, and notice will be given within the first six months that the works are going to be commenced, in order that the commissioner or commissioners referred to in the first part of the preceding article, may be present to inspect the works that may be executed.

Surveys, &c., submitted within eighteen months. Notice of commencement within six months thereafter.

"Art. 8.—La compañía La-Sère comenzará la construccion del ferrocarril y linea telegráfica, dentro de seis meses, contados despues del año y medio de que habla el artículo anterior, debiendo terminar en cada año, á satisfaccion del Gobierno, un tramo de quince leguas por lo ménos, hasta la conclusion de toda la linea, que será precisamente tres años despues del dia en que empezaron los trabajos. Las quince leguas que la compañía está obligada á dejar construidas anualmente, podrán serlo en tramos aislados unos de otros, con tal que no se separen del trayecto general aprobado por el Ejecutivo.

"Art. 9.—La compañía comenzará la construccion del camino carretero al mismo tiempo que la del ferrocarril, y la terminará á satisfaccion del Gobierno dentro de un año y medio á lo mas, contado desde la fecha fijada para comenzarlos.

"Art. 10.—De los terrenos baldíos que hubiere, el Gobierno dá á la compañía la faja que necesitare para la linea de los caminos, y ademas la mitad de los baldíos que se encuentren dentro de una legua lateral por cada lado de solo el ferrocarril, en todo el espacio que recorra. Dichos terrenos baldíos se dividirán donde su extension lo permita, en cuadros de una legua cada uno; y en donde tuvieren ménos de dos leguas en su longitud á lo largo del camino (ó en las fracciones de ménos de dos leguas), se dividirán por mitad, perteneciendo una á la Nacion y otra á la compañía. Las porciones divididas se numerarán en cada lado, comenzando en ambos por el número 1 en el Norte, y siguiendo en el órden numérico hácia el Sur; de manera que el número 1 del lado de Occidente, ó sea el lado derecho del camino, quede frente del número 1 del lado de Oriente ó lado izquierdo, á no ser que pasando el camino por lugares en que por un solo lado haya baldíos dentro de la linea lateral, hubiere puntos de interseccion en terrenos de propiedad particular, en

Construction to be begun within two years. Fifteen leagues to be completed each year, and whole line in three years.

Article 8th.—The La Sère Company shall commence the construction of the railroad and telegraph line within six months, counted after the year and a half mentioned in the preceding article, and the company is to complete within each year, to the satisfaction of the Government, a section of at least fifteen leagues, until the completion of the whole line, which must be precisely three years from the day on which the works were commenced. The fifteen leagues which the company is obliged to construct annually, may be made by it in sections separate from each other, provided that they should not be apart from the general line of road approved by the Executive.

Carriage-road to be built within a year and a half.

Article 9th.—The company shall commence the construction of the carriage road at the same time as that of the railroad, and shall complete the former to the satisfaction of the Government within a year and a half at the utmost, counting from the date fixed for its commencement.

Grant of unclaimed lands along line, and one half of those within a league on each side.

Article 10th.—Of the unclaimed lands that may exist, the Government gives to the company the strip that it may require for the line of the roads, and besides this, the half of the unclaimed lands (which may be found within a lateral league) on each side of the railroad only, through the whole length of its line Said unclaimed lands will be divided, where their extent will allow, into squares of a league each; and where they cover less than two leagues longitudinally along the side of the road (or the fractions of less than two leagues), will be divided into halves, one belonging to the Nation and the other to the company. The portions divided will be numbered on each side, commencing on both by No. 1 on the north, and following in numerical order toward the south, so that No. 1 on the western side, or be it the right side of the road, should be opposite to No. 1 on the eastern or left side, unless the road should pass through places where only on one side of it there should be unclaimed lands, within the lateral line, where there

cuyo caso quedará interrumpido el órden expresado, siguiendo luego hasta el fin del camino la numeracion prescrita para las porciones del terreno por ambos lados.

"ART. 11.—La Nacion se reserva desde luego, en pleno dominio, en el lado occidental ó derecho del camino, todas las porciones señaladas con los números impares 1, 3, 5, &c., y de la misma manera se reserva en el lado oriental ó izquierdo del camino, todas las porciones marcadas con los números pares 2, 4, 6, &c., cediendo á los concesionarios en propiedad, revocable solo en el caso de que no concluyan el camino, las porciones señaladas con los números pares en el lado occidental ó derecho del camino, y las porciones marcadas con los números impares en el lado oriental ó izquierdo. Si por el caso de interseccion enunciado en el artículo anterior, se encontraren mas porciones de terrenos baldíos en un lado del camino que en el otro, los que hubiere de exceso en cualquiera de los dos lados, serán divididos por mitad entre la Nacion y los concesionarios; de manera que se observen siempre precisamente de legua en legua, las dos alternativas, de lado y de frente, entre las porciones nacionales y las de la empresa.

"ART. 12.—El Gobierno concede á la compañia, si lo hubiere, el terreno para los muelles, diques y otras obras indispensables en los puertos de Goatzacoalcos y de la Ventosa, comprometiéndose la compañia á construir por su cuenta, á satisfaccion del Gobierno, en los dos años siguientes á la fecha en que se construya el ferrocarril, dichos muelles y diques; haciendo desde luego las obras precisas para facilitar la descarga de los buques y evitar la avería de las mercancías.

"ART. 13.—La compañía tomará gratis de las tierras que fueren del dominio público, por el tiempo que lo fueren, sin que esto importe para el Gobierno la obligacion de no enagenarlas, en todo ó en parte, los

might be points of intersection on lands of private property, in which case the said order would be interrupted, and afterwards the prescribed numeration continuing to the end of the road, for the portions of land on both sides.

Reservation of one-half of the land on each side of road by Government.

ARTICLE 11TH.—The Nation reserves for itself, in full dominion, all the portions on the western or right side of the road marked with the odd numbers 1, 3, 5, &c., and in like manner reserves for itself on the eastern, or left side of the road, all the portions marked with the even numbers, 2, 4, 6, &c., ceding to the grantees in proprietorship, revokable only in case that they should not finish the road, all the portions marked with the even numbers on the western or right side of the road, and the portions marked with the odd numbers on the eastern or left side. If, in case of intersection as specified in the preceding article, there should be found more portions of unclaimed lands on one side of the road than on the other, those that should be in excess on either of the two sides, will be divided in halves between the Nation and the grantees, so that the two alternatives of side and frontage be exactly observed from league to league between the National portion and that of the company.

Cession of Government land for wharves to be constructed in two years after completion of road.

ARTICLE 12TH.—The Government cedes to the company such ground as it may own, for wharves, docks, and other indispensable works, in the ports of Goatzacoalcos and Ventosa, the company engaging to construct said wharves and docks at its own cost, to the satisfaction of the Government, in the two years following the date in which the railroad will be constructed; making at once the necessary works to facilitate the discharge of vessels, and to avoid damage to merchandise.

Company to have from Government land materials for roads, wharves, &c.

ARTICLE 13TH.—The company may take, gratis, from the lands which may be of public domain, for the time that they may be so, without implying thereby any obligation on the part of the Government, not to

materiales necesarios para la construccion y conservacion de los caminos, telégrafos, muelles, diques ó de sus pertenencias

"Art. 14.—Los terrenos y materiales de propiedad particular que necesitare la compañia, los tomará indemnizando á sus dueños conforme á las leyes.

"Art. 15—La compañía tendrá obligacion de construir y conservar faros de primera clase en donde fuere mas conveniente á los dos extremos de la vía, debiendo quedar concluidos dentro de tres años despues de terminado el ferrocarril, los que serán de la pertenencia exclusiva del Gobierno.

"Art. 16.—A los sesenta dias de la fecha de esta ley, la compañía dará una fianza por valor de cien mil pesos fuertes, á satisfaccion del ministro de México en Washington ó de quien le supliere, siendo indispensable esta condicion para la existencia y validez de las concesiones hechas por este decreto, y perdiendo los concesionarios la expresada suma en caso de que no cumplan dentro de los plazos señalados las obligaciones de presentar los planos y de comenzar y acabar los caminos y linea telegráfica. Con la mencionada fianza se asegurará tambien la obligacion que contrae la compañía de acreditar que está organizada ya conforme á las leyes de uno de los Estados de la Union Americana.

"Art. 17.—Durante el tiempo necesario para la construccion del ferrocarril, la compañía podrá importar al Istmo, libres de derechos, los materiales, máquinas, herramientas, carbon de piedra, carruages y útiles necesarios para la construccion de la via y de sus pertenencias. Pasado el término de la construccion del camino, solo podrá introducir, libres de derechos, las máquinas, carbon de piedra, carros y rieles que necesitare, durando esta exencion por espacio de setenta años, y haciendo la compañía uso de ella, así como de

sell or alienate them, in whole or in part, the materials necessary for the construction and repairs of the roads, telegraphs, wharves, docks, or their appurtenances.

Private property to be taken, but owners indemnified.

ARTICLE 14TH.—The lands and materials of private property, which may be needed by the company, will be taken by it, indemnifying the owners in conformity with the laws.

Light-houses to be built by company within three years after railroad, and to belong to Government.

ARTICLE 15TH.—The company will be obliged to construct and keep in repair light-houses of first class, where most desirable, at the extreme ends of the road, which are to be finished within three years from the termination of the building of the railroad; said light-houses remaining as the exclusive property of the Government.

Company to give bond in $100,000 to complete road and telegraph line within prescribed time.

ARTICLE 16TH.—Sixty days from the date of this law, the company will give a bond in the sum of one hundred thousand dollars coin, satisfactory to the Mexican Minister at Washington, or to whomsoever may fill his place, this condition being indispensable for the existence and validity of the concessions made by this decree, and the grantees forfeiting the said sum, in case of non-compliance within the terms of time marked, with the obligations to present the plans and to commence and finish the roads and telegraph line. With the said bond the obligation will be insured, which the company contracts to accredit, that it is already organized according to the laws of one of the States of the American Union.

Exemption from duty granted for importation of materials for building and running road.

ARTICLE 17TH.—During the time necessary for the construction of the railroad, the company shall have the right to import on the Isthmus, free of duties, the materials, machinery, tools, mineral coal, carriages, and necessary utensils for the construction of the road and its appurtenances. After the expiration of the time fixed for the construction of the road, it will only be allowed to introduce, free of duty, the machines, mineral coal, cars and rails, which it may require; this exemption lasting for the space of seventy years, and the company making use of it, as well as of

la anterior, segun las reglas que se dicten por el ministerio de hacienda.

"Art. 18.—La compañía tiene obligacion de limpiar el rio Goatzacoalcos en la parte de él que dedique á la navegacion.

"Art. 19—Se concede á la compañía la facultad de cobrar peages, derechos de tránsito, de muelles, de almacenage y cualesquiera otros, por fletes de mercancías, conduccion de pasageros y trasmision de telégramas; pero la tarifa que se fije por la compañía para la suma en junto de todos esos derechos, excepto solamente el de almacenage, no excederá de cincuenta centavos por legua para cada pasagero, de tres centavos por legua para cada arroba de mercancías, de uno por ciento del valor de los metales preciosos y de alhajas, entendiéndose esta asignacion para toda la travesía del camino por tierra y por agua; y de diez centavos por cada palabra de los telégramas.

"Art. 20.—El Gobierno no exigirá, durante los setenta años de la concesion, impuesto ni contribucion alguna, ya sea sobre las mercancías que pasen solo de tránsito por el Istmo, ya sea de los pasageros, ya sea de los telégramas, ó ya, en fin, sobre los capitales invertidos en los caminos y linea telegráfica, y en toda la empresa. Las mercancías que se consuman en puntos del Istmo, ó que se extraigan de ellos, no disfrutarán de esta exencion.

"Art. 21.—Respecto de la linea de tránsito que se forme entre los puertos de Goatzacoalcos y la Ventosa, ó del puerto que se elija en el Pacífico, en parte por agua, y en parte por el ferrocarril, el Gobierno se obliga á no otorgar á otra compañía, durante los setenta años mencionados, las concesiones especificades en esta ley; entendiéndose, respecto del cobro de impuestos, que á ninguna otra compañía se dispensará ni rebajará el pago de los derechos que debieren satisfacer con arreglo á los aranceles que estuvieren vigentes en las aduanas marítimas.

the former one, according to the rules that may be dictated by the Minister of Finance.

River to be cleared.

ARTICLE 18TH.—The company is obliged to clear that part of the Goatzacoalcos River which it may use for navigation.

Company's tariff limited.

ARTICLE 19TH.—The right is conceded to the company to collect portages and transit-fees, wharfage, storage, and any other fees for freight on merchandise, transportation of passengers, and transmission of telegrams; but the tariff which the company may establish for the sum total of all its fees, wharfage alone excepted, will not exceed fifty cents per league for each passenger, three cents per league for each arroba (25 lbs.) of merchandise, one per cent on the value of precious metals and jewels, this assignment being understood to be for the whole transit of the route by land and water, and ten cents for each word of the telegrams.

No tax on through traffic.

ARTICLE 20TH.—The Government will not exact during the seventy years of the concession, any impost or contribution, be it on the merchandise which may pass only on transit through the Isthmus, be it on the the passengers, be it on the telegrams, or be it, in fine, on the capital expended on the roads and telegraphic line, and in the whole enterprise. The merchandise which may be consumed in points on the Isthmus, or exported therefrom, shall not enjoy this exemption.

No similar concessions and exemptions to any other company.

ARTICLE 21ST.—With respect to the line of transit that may be established between the ports of Goatzacoalcos and Ventosa, or such Pacific port as may be chosen, partly by water and partly by railroad, the Government obligates itself not to grant to any other company during the said seventy years, the concessions specified in this law. It being understood, in regard to the collection of imposts, that no other company will be exempted from, or have any reduction made, in the payment of the duties as exacted by the tariffs which may be in force in the maritime custom houses.

"Art. 22.—El Gobierno protejerá la prosecucion, conservacion y seguridad de los trabajos, con toda la fuerza que estimare conveniente para una obra de grande y notoria utilidad pública.

"Art. 23.—El Gobierno conservará abiertos y habilitados para el comercio de altura, durante los setenta años de la concesion, el puerto de Goatzacoalcos en el Golfo de México, y en el Pacífico el de la Ventosa ó cualquiera otro que se creyere mas conveniente que este.

"Art. 24.—La facultad concedida á la compañía para el trasporte de mercancías, se reglamentará por el Ministerio de Hacienda, procurando evitar los abusos y facilitar la pronta expedicion de aquellas; sin que se entienda por dicha facultad que la compañía tiene derecho de abrir expendio de mercancías en ningun punto del Istmo.

"Art. 25.—Las concesiones hechas á la compañía durarán setenta años, contados desde que el ferrocarril y telégrafo se pongan al servicio público; y en todo ese tiempo el Gobierno recibirá un 8 por ciento de las utilidades líquidas de la empresa, siempre que se hagan dividendos á los accionistas, y bajo el concepto, de que luego que haya utilidades, se hará por lo ménos un dividendo anual. Tambien percibirá el Gobierno, mediante liquidacion y pago por meses, doce centavos por cada uno de los pasegeros que transiten por la vía general.

"Art. 26.—Al espirar el plazo de la concesion, tendrá el Gobierno mexicano el derecho de adquirir la propiedad del ferrocarril con sus estaciones, telégrafos, muelles, diques, útiles y pertenencias, por el avalúo que de ellos hicieren dos peritos nombrados uno por el Gobierno y otro por la compañía, ó por un tercero designado por los primeros en caso de discordia.

Si el Gobierno no usare del derecho que le concede la fraccion anterior, la compañía La-Sère continuará

ARTICLE 22D.—The Government will protect the prosecution, preservation, and safety of the works with all the force that it may deem desirable for a great work of notorious public utility. Government protection granted.

ARTICLE 23D.—The Government will keep open as ports of entry during the seventy years of the grant, the port of Goatzacoalcos, on the Gulf of Mexico, and of Ventosa, on the Pacific, or any other port that may be deemed preferable. Certain ports of entry to be kept open.

ARTICLE 24TH.—The privilege granted to the company for the transportation of merchandise will be regulated by the Minister of Finance, trying to prevent abuses, and to facilitate its quick transmission; nor by said privilege is it to be construed that the company has the right to open the sale of merchandise on any point of the Isthmus. Minister of Finance to regulate privileges.

ARTICLE 25TH.—The concessions made to the company will continue for seventy years, counting from the time when the railroad and telegraph are placed in the public service, and during all that time the Government will receive eight per cent of the net profits of the enterprise, whenever dividends shall be declared for the stockholders, and with the understanding that as soon as there may be profits, one annual dividend, at least, will be declared. The Government will also receive, in monthly settlement and payment, twelve cents for each passenger going over the general road. Concessions for seventy years. Government to receive eight per cent from profits, and twelve cents for each passenger.

ARTICLE 26TH.—On the expiration of the term of this grant the Mexican Government shall have the right to acquire the proprietorship of the railroad, with its stations, telegraphs, wharves, docks, tools, and appurtenances, for the valuation that may be made by two experts, one named by the Government, and the other by the company, or by a third, appointed by the former, in case of disagreement. After grant expires Government may take railroad at valuation.

Should the Government not use the right given to it by the previous clause, the La Sère Company will

gozando la propiedad y posesion del camino con todas sus obras y material; pero cesarán las exenciones que le concede esta ley, y seguirá pagando al Gobierno el 8 por ciento de las utilidades líquidas, y los doce centavos por pasagero en los términos que el artículo anterior lo previene.

"Art. 27.—La compañía estará obligada á llevar á cualquier punto, en todo el tránsito del camino, libres de gastos, la correspondencia é impresos que transiten por él, y á que dé curso la oficina respectiva, recibiéndolos y entregándolos con las formalidades debidas. De la misma manera trasportará todos los frutos y objetos que sean de propiedad del Gobierno, por la mitad de la tarifa. Igualmente conducirá sin estipendio alguno, los oficiales, tropas, empleados ó agentes del Gobierno general ó de los Estados, cuando caminen por causa del servicio público. Trasmitirá tambien, libres de gastos, por su linea telegráfica, todos los mensages enviados por funcionarios ó empleados de la República mexicana, ó de cualquiera de sus Estados, sobre negocios públicos. Los metales y productos agrícolos é industriales de la República, serán trasportados por un 30 por ciento ménos del precio de tarifa, sujetándose á las reglas que se dicten por el Ministerio de Hacienda.

"Art. 28.—El tránsito por la vía de comunicacion será libre para todos los habítantes del globo; pero se aumentará un 25 por ciento á las mercancías de las naciones que no tuvieren tratado de neutralidad con México, respecto del tránsito del Istmo.

"Art. 29.—La compañía tendrá facultad de trasportar en balijas cerradas, que no podrán abrirse, la correspondencia extrangera, por la via de comunicacion; y dichas balijas serán selladas por la administracion de correos, ó la de las aduanas marítimas.

continue enjoying the proprietorship and possession of the road, with all its works and material; but the exemptions granted by this law will cease, and it will continue paying to the Government the eight per cent. of the net profits, and the twelve cents per passenger, according to the terms specified in the preceding article.

Mails, &c., to be carried free, Government property at half rates.

ARTICLE 27TH.—The company will be obliged to carry to any point on the whole line of the road, free of charges, the correspondence and printed matter sent by it from the respective post offices, and the company will receive and deliver the same with the due formalities. The company will also carry, for half tariff rates, all the freight and property of the Government. Also, the company will give free transportation to the officers, troops, employees, and agents of the General Government, or of the State Governments when traveling for purposes of public service. It also will transmit, free of charge, by its telegraphic line, all the messages sent by functionaries or employees of the Mexican Republic, or any of its States, on public matters. The metals, agricultural and industrial products of the Republic, will be transported at a reduction of thirty per cent. less than the tariff rates, and be subject to the regulations that may be dictated by the Minister of Finance.

Transit open to all nations.

ARTICLE 28TH.—The transit by this route of communication will be open to all the inhabitants of the globe, but will be increased twenty-five per cent. on the merchandise of the nations not having a treaty of neutrality with Mexico with regard to the transit of the Isthmus.

Foreign mails to be in sealed bags.

ARTICLE 29TH.—The company will have the privilege of transporting by this route foreign correspondence, in closed mail bags, which must not be opened; and said mail bags will be sealed by the postmasters, or the collectors of the maritime customs.

"Art. 30.—El Gobierno nombrará la cuarta parte de los directores de la compañia, y los nombrados por él tendrán las mismas facultades y prerogativas que los otros; podrá tambien constituir en el Istmo una comision que vigile las obras y trabajos que se emprendan en virtud de este contrato.

"Art. 31.—Los vapores ó buques de la compañía tendrán derecho de navegar en el rio de Goatzacoalcos, durante los setenta años de la concesion, haciéndolo precisamente con bandera mexicana, y estando obligados á tener la dotacion de oficiales y tripulaciones que las leyes requieren para los buques nacionales, formándola con mexicanos por nacimiento ó por naturalizacion. Para el segundo caso se darán á la compañía las cartas de naturalizacion que pida.

"Art. 32.—La concesion otorgada en el artículo anterior, no se opone á que otros buques y vapores naveguen en el rio Goatzacoalcos, para el comercio y cualesquiera otros objetos, siempre que esa navegacion sea arreglada á las leyes de la República mexicana.

"Art. 33.—Los buques de la compañía que conduzcan únicamente pasageros, correspondencia y mercancías para el tránsito de toda la via, estarán exentos del derecho de toneladas. Si condujeren ademas mercancias para algun punto del Istmo, pagarán el derecho de toneladas por solo lo relativo á esas mismas mercancías, y no por lo demas.

"Art. 34.—La compañía se hará cargo de pagar lo que legal y justamente pueda deberse del préstamo que Mr. Francisco P. Falconett hizo á la empresa Sloo, continuando el Gobierno libre de toda responsabilidad futura respecto de ese préstamo, y sin que por esto se disminuya la parte de utilidades que le pertenezcan de los productos del camino.

ARTICLE 30TH.—The Government will name one-fourth of the number of the directors of the company, and those named by it will have the same rights and prerogatives as the others. It will also have the right to appoint a commission on the Isthmus to watch the works and operations that may be undertaken in virtue of this contract.

Government may appoint one-fourth of directors.

ARTICLE 31ST.—The steamers and vessels of the company shall have the right to navigate the Goatzacoalcos River, during the seventy years of the concession, doing it necessarily under the Mexican flag, and being obliged to have the muster of officers and crew that the law requires for national vessels, forming it with Mexicans by birth or by naturalization. In the latter case, letters of naturalization will be given whenever the company may demand.

Right to navigate River.

ARTICLE 32D.—The privilege granted in the preceding article is not to conflict with the navigation of the Goatzacoalcos River by other steamers and vessels, for purposes of trade or otherwise, which vessels, in their navigation, are to observe the existing laws of the Mexican Republic.

Not to conflict with right of other vessels.

ARTICLE 33D.—The company's vessels, carrying exclusively passengers, correspondence, and merchandise, for the transit of the whole route, shall be exempt from tonnage duty. Should they, besides, carry merchandise for any point on the Isthmus, they will pay tonnage duty only on that portion appropriated for said merchandise, and no more.

No tonnage duty for through transportation.

ARTICLE 34TH.—The company will undertake to pay whatever may be legally and justly due on the loan that Mr. Francis P. Falconet made to the Sloo Enterprise, the Government to continue free from all responsibility in future with respect to said loan, and without diminishing for that reason the part of the profits that may belong to it out of the proceeds of the road.

Company responsible for Falconet loan.

" Art. 35.—La empresa á que esta ley se refiere, es y será siempre exclusivamente mexicana; y la compañía de La-Sère para el tránsito de Tehuantepec, aun cuando se forme en el extrangero, se considerará, sin embargo, como constituida ahora en la República mexicana, cual si en ella misma se hubiere formado y organizado, con arreglo á las leyes mexicanas; pero si estimare oportuno constituir compañías separadas, bajo las razones sociales que escoja, para cada uno ó para varios de los ramos comprendidos en las operaciones que debe ejecutar, podrá instituir tales compañías, formándolas y organizándolas, ya sea en la república, ya en los Estados-Unidos, conforme á la leyes generales ó especiales del lugar en que las instituya, aunque siempre deberán ser consideradas como dependientes en todo de la misma compañía principal, exclusivamente mexicana, y sujetas en consecuencia á las prescripciones de esta ley.

" Art. 36.—En virtud de lo provenido en el artículo anterior, la compañía La-Sère, y cualquiera otra que pueda sucederle, así como todos los extrangeros y los sucesores de estos que tomen parte en la empresa, sea como accionistas, empleados, ó con cualquiera otro título ó carácter, serán considerados como mexicanos en todo lo que á dicha empresa se refiera; no podrán alegar respecto de los titulos relacionados con la empresa, derechos de extrangería; solo tendrán en caso de denegacion de justicia, los mismos derechos y medios de hacerlos valer en todo lo concerniente á la empresa, que los que las leyes de la República conceden á los mexicanos; y no podrán hacer valer dichos derechos sino ante los tribunales mexicanos.

" Art. 37.—Las restricciones del artículo anterior no tendrán lugar en las discusiones ó diferencias que se susciten entre extrangeros accionistas, y fuera de la República, en cuyo caso se podrán examinar y decidir como si las restricciones no existiesen; pero sin que las

Article 35th.—The enterprise to which this law refers, is, and will ever be exclusively Mexican, and the La Sère Company for the transit of Tehuantepec, though it may be formed abroad, will be considered, nothwithstanding, as now constituted within the Mexican Republic, as much so as if it had been formed and organized within it according to the Mexican laws; but if he should deem it opportune to organize different companies, with the titles or names that he may elect, for the purpose of carrying out one or more of the objects comprehended in the operations that he hereby undertakes, he can constitute such companies, forming and organizing them, be it in this Republic, or be it in the United States, in conformity with the general or special laws of the place where he constitutes them, though they are always to be considered as dependencies of the one principal company, exclusively Mexican, and consequently subject to the prescriptions of this decree.

Company to be a Mexican organization, but to have the privilege of forming other companies in Mexico or the United States.

Article 36th.—In virtue of the provisions of the preceding article, the La Sère Company, and any other which may succeed it, as also all the foreigners and their successors who may take part in the enterprise, whether as stockholders, employees, or under any other title or character, will be regarded as Mexicans in all that concerns said enterprise—they shall not bring forward any claims based on their rights as foreigners in any matter connected with said enterprise; and in case of appeal for redress, they shall only have the same rights and means of asserting them, in anything concerning the enterprise, that the laws of the Republic grant to Mexicans, and they shall only make good their said rights before the Mexican tribunals.

All engaged now or hereafter in company to be regarded as Mexicans.

Article 37th.—The restrictions contained in the preceding article shall not be operative in any controversies or differences that may arise between foreign stockholders, out of the republic, in which case they may be examined and adjudged as if the said restric-

Actions of foreign tribunals in respect to company not to affect this decree.

decisiones de los tribunàles extrangeros afecten en manera alguna á las prescripciones de este decreto, á la compañía La-Sère, la cual se reputa mexicana para todos los efectos del mismo decreto, y á los intereses mexicanos.

"Art. 38.—La compañía que forme La-Sère, no podrá traspasar, ni enagenar, ni hipotecar las concesiones de esta ley, ni el ferrocarril, ni el telégrafo, ni los diques y muelles, sin consentimiento previo del Gobierno general, y en ningun caso podrá traspasar, ni enagenar, ni hipotecar las concesiones, ni el ferrocarril, ni el telégrafo, ni los diques y muelles, á ningun Gobierno extrangero, siendo nula y de ningun valor la enagenacion ó hipoteca que se hiciere. Tampoco podrá la compañía admitir en ningun caso como socio á un Gobierno ó Estado extrangero, siendo igualmente nula y de ningun valor cualquiera estipulacion que hiciere en este sentido. Se autoriza, sin embargo, á la compañía para que sin la aprobacion del Gobierno pueda expedir y vender bonos y obligaciones, cuándo, en las cantidades y por el precio que juzgare conveniente, y para asegurar el pago, hipotecando solo el ferrocarril, linea telegráfica, estaciones, muelles, diques y demas obras, con tal que la hipoteca no se extienda á la concesion, y que se concluya á favor de individuos ó asociaciones particulares.

"Art. 39.—D. Emilio La-Sère podrá establecer en Nueva-York ó en cualquiera otro punto de los Estados-Unidos, la junta directiva de la compañía, contrayendo la obligacion de constituir en México un apoderado, amplia y suficientemente autorizado, y con las instrucciones necesarias para entenderse con el Gobierno general y demas autoridades de la República, en todos los negocios que se refieren á las obligaciones que le impone este decreto á la empresa.

"Art. 40.—Se permite á la compañía que forme La-Sère, establecer á su costa en el puerto de Huatul-

tions did not exist. But the actions of foreign tribunals are not to affect in any way the provisions of this decree, as towards the La Sère Company, which shall be reputed Mexican for all the effects of said decree and as Mexican interests.

No sale of road, &c., without Government consent. Sale to foreign government prohibited. How Bonds may be issued and property hypothecated.

ARTICLE 38TH.—The company to be formed by La Sère shall not transfer, sell, alienate, or hypothecate the concessions of this law, nor the railroad nor the telegraph, nor the docks and wharves, without the previous consent of the General Government, and under no circumstances will it be able to transfer, sell, or hypothecate the concessions, or railroad, or telegraph, or docks and wharves, to any foreign government; such sale, alienation, or hypothecation would of itself be a nullity and of no value. Neither shall the company admit, in any event, as associate, a foreign government or State; any stipulation which might be made in this sense would be equally null and of no value. The company is, however, authorized, without the approbation of the Government, to issue and sell bonds and obligations, when, in amounts and for the price it may deem advisable, and to secure payment by hypothecating only the railroad, telegraphic line, stations, wharves, docks and other works; provided, that the hypothecation should not extend to the grant, and that it should be made to individuals or private associations.

Board of directors may be in United States.

ARTICLE 39TH.—Don Emilio La Sère has power to establish in New York, or in any other place of the United States, the board of directors of the company, contracting the obligation to appoint a representative in Mexico, fully and sufficiently empowered, and furnished with the necessary instructions to treat with the General Government and other authorities of the Republic on all matters which may refer to the obligations that this decree imposes on the enterprise.

Depot for coal and navy yard in Huatulco.

ARTICLE 40TH.—Permission is given to the company to be formed by La Sère to establish, at its cost, in the port of Huatulco, a depot for mineral

co, un depósito de carbon de piedra y un astillero, que estará bajo la immediata vigilancia de la autoridad, para la reparacion de los vapores que se ocupen en la conduccion de pasageros y mercancías por el Istmo; pero sin que en ningun caso se entienda concedida la propiedad del terreno destinado á tales establecimientos.

"Art. 41 —Las obligaciones que contrae La-Sère respecto de los plazos fijados en esta ley, se suspenderán en todo caso fortuito ó de fuerza mayor, que impida directa y absolutamente el cumplimiento de tales obligaciones; y la suspension durará solo por el tiempo que dure el impedimento. D. Emilio La-Sère deberá presentar al Gobierno general las noticias y pruebas de haber ocurrido un caso fortuito ó de fuerza mayor, del carácter mencionado, dentro del término de tres meses de haber comenzado el impedimento; y por solo el hecho de no presentar tales noticias y pruebas dentro del término señalado, no podrá ya La-Sère alegar en ningun tiempo la circumstancia de caso fortuito ó de fuerza mayor. Igualmente deberá presentar La-Sère al Gobierno general las noticias y pruebas de que los trabajos han continuado en el acto de cesar el impedimento, ó á lo ménos dentro de dos meses despues de haber cesado, haciéndose la expresada presentacion dentro de los dos meses siguientes á los dos mencionados. Solamente se abonará á D. Emilio La-Sère el tiempo que hubiere durado el impedimento, ó á lo sumo dos meses mas.

"Art. 42.—Se imponen á la compañía La-Sère las restricciones siguientes:

"*Primera.* No podrá construir ninguna fortaleza en el Istmo.

"*Segunda.* No podrá organizar fuerza armada de ninguna clase; pero los empleados de la compañía podrán estar armados para su defensa personal.

coal, and a ship yard, which will be under the immediate vigilance of the authority, for the repair of steamers which may be engaged in the transportation of passengers and merchandise to and from the Isthmus; but in no event is it to be understood that the proprietorship of the grounds used for such establishments is conceded.

Obligations as to time suspended during operation of "force majeure."

ARTICLE 41ST.—The obligations contracted by La Sère, with respect to the terms of time fixed by this law, will be suspended in any fortuitous case, or of "force majeure," which may prevent, directly or absolutely, compliance with said obligations, and the suspension will continue only for the time the impediment lasts. Don Emilio La Sère shall present to the General Government the notices and proof of a fortuitous case, or of "force majeure," of the character mentioned having occurred within the term of three months from the commencement of the impediment, and for the sole fact of not presenting such notices and proofs within the term specified, La Sère will not be able any longer to allege, at any time, the circumstance of a fortuitous case, or case of "force majeure." La Sère shall also present to the General Government the notices and proofs that the works were resumed immediately on the cessation of the impediments, or at least within two months from the time of such cessation, and notice of such fact will have to be made within two months from the termination of the two just mentioned. All that will be allowed to Don Emilio La Sère will be the time of the duration of the impediment, or, at the utmost, two months more.

Restrictions.

ARTICLE 42D.—The following restrictions are imposed on the La Sère Company:

No fort to be built on Isthmus.

First. It shall not construct any fort on the Isthmus.

No armed force to be organized.

Second. It shall not organize an armed force of any kind, but the employees of the company may be armed for their personal defense.

" *Tercera.* No podrá dar passage á fuerza alguna armada extrangera, sin expresa autorizacion del Gobierno general.

" *Cuarta.* No podrá conducir ningunos efectos de un beligerante, declarados contrabando de guerra por las leyes de la República mexicana, sin expresa autorizacion del Gobierno general.

" *Quinta.* No podrá dar pasage á fuerza alguna armada nacional, ni conducir municiones ó pertrechos de guerra nacionales, sin expresa autorizacion del Gobierno general, ó de otra autoridad competente.

" *Sexta.* Despedirá inmediatamente de su servicio á cualquiera de sus dependientes que haga ó proteja el contrabando, ó que cometa cualquier delito, y auxiliará al Gobierno para su persecucion.

" *Setima.* Pondrá en ejecucion los medios que se le designen por el Gobierno general, para que todo pasagero observe las leyes aduanales de la República.

" Art. 43.—Las concesiones otorgadas en la presente ley, caducarán por las causas siguientes:

" *Primera.* Por no dar la fianza dentro de noventa dias contados desde la fecha de esta ley, por valor de ($100,000) cien mil pesos, de que habla el art. 16.

" *Segunda.* Por no cumplir las obligaciones relativas á la presentacion de los planos y á la construccion de los tramos y de todo el camino, dentro de los plazos fijados al efecto en esta ley.

" *Tercera.* Por construir alguna fortaleza en el Istmo de Tehuantepec.

" *Cuarta.* Por organizar fuerza armada de cualquiera clase que sea, sin comprender en esto á los empleados armados para su defensa personal.

Third. It shall not give passage to any foreign armed force without an express authorization from the General Government.

No foreign armed force to be carried.

Fourth. It shall not carry any effects of a belligerent, declared contraband of war by the laws of the Mexican Republic, without an express authorization from the General Government.

No contraband of war to be carried.

Fifth. It shall not give passage to any national armed force, nor to carry national ammunition or articles of war, without express authorization from the General Government or from some other competent authority.

Transportation of national armed force and war materials subject to Government authority.

Sixth. It shall immediately discharge from its service any of its subordinates who smuggle or protect smuggling, or commit any crime, and shall co-operate with the Government in the prosecution of the same.

Smugglers and criminals to be discharged from company's employ.

Seventh. It shall execute all the measures that the General Government may designate, in order that all passengers may observe the revenue laws of the Republic.

Measures as to revenue laws to be observed.

ARTICLE 43D.—The privileges granted by this decree will be forfeited for any of the following reasons:

Forfeiture of privileges.

First. For failing to give, within ninety days, counted from the date of this decree, the security for one hundred thousand dollars, as mentioned in Article 16.

In default of bond.

Second. For failing to comply with the obligations of this decree relative to the presentation of the plans, and to the construction of the sections of the road, and of the whole road, within the terms of time as fixed by this law.

For failure to present plans and construct road within time limited.

Third. For constructing any fort on the Isthmus of Tehuantepec.

For constructing fort on Isthmus.

Fourth. For organizing an armed force, whatever its character may be, but this does not include the employees of the company, who may be armed for their personal defense.

For organizing an armed force.

" *Quinta.* Por dar pasage á cualquiera fuerza armada extrangera, sin expresa autorizacion del Gobierno general, excepto en el caso de fuerza mayor, plenamente justificado.

" *Sexta.* Por conducir, sin expresa autorizacion del Gobierno general, efectos de alguna potencia beligerante, de los declarados contrabando de guerra por las leyes de la República mexicana.

" *Setima.* Por dar pasage á cualquiera fuerza armada nacional, ó conducir municiones ó pertrechos de guerra nacionales, sin expresa autorizacion del Gobierno general, ó de otra autoridad competente, á no ser que haya fuerza mayor, plenamente justificada.

" *Octava.* Por suspender durante un año consecutivo los trabajos en el camino, ó por dos años cuando se haya empleado en el ferrocarril y demas obras un millon de pesos por lo ménos.

" *Novena.* Por infringir cualquiera de las cláusulas de esta ley, en las que se previene que no podrá la compañia La Sère traspasar, ni enagenar, ni hipotecar las concesiones de la misma ley, ni el ferrocarril ni el telégrafo, ni los muelles y diques, sin previo consentimiento, del Gobierno general; y que en ningun caso podrá traspasar, ni enagenar, ni hipotecar las concesiones, ni el ferrocarril, ni el telégrafo, ni los muelles y diques á ningun gobierno ó Estado extrangero; no pudiendo tampoco en ningun caso, admitir como socio á ningun Gobierno ó Estado extrangero.

" Art. 44.—En caso de que la compañía faltare á las otras obligaciones ó restricciones que le impone esta ley, quedará sujeta á la reparacion de la falta, y á la correspondiente indemnizacion.

" Art. 45.—En cualquiera de los casos especifi cados en el artículo 42, perderá la compañía las concesiones otorgadas en esta ley, de las cuales podrá

Fifth. For giving passage to any foreign armed force without express authorization from the General Government, except in the case of overpowering force, fully justified.

For unauthorized transportation of foreign armed force.

Sixth. For carrying, without express authorization from the General Government, effects of any belligerent power of those declared by the laws of the Mexican Republic contraband of war.

For carrying articles contraband of war.

Seventh. For giving passage to any National armed force, or carrying National ammunition or articles of war, without an express authorization from the General Government or other competent authority, unless done under the compulsion of superior force, fully justified.

For carrying National armies without consent.

Eighth. For suspending during one consecutive year the works on the road; or for two years, when one million of dollars, at least, have been expended on the railroad, and other works.

For suspension of work for one or two years.

Ninth. For violating any of the clauses of this decree in which it is provided that the La Sère Company shall not transfer, sell, alienate, or hypothecate the concessions of this same law, nor the railroad, nor telegraph, nor the wharves and docks, without the previous consent of the General Government, and that in no event shall it transfer, sell, alienate, or hypothecate the concessions, railroad, telegraph, wharves, and docks to any foreign government or State, nor in any event admit as associate any foreign government or State.

For transfer of rights and property without consent of Government.

Article 44th.—In case the company should fail to comply with any of the other obligations or restrictions which this law imposes, it shall be subject to the reparation of the fault, and to the corresponding indemnity.

Company liable for non-compliance with other obligations.

Article 45th.—In any of the cases specified in Article 42d the company will forfeit the privileges granted by this law, and the Government will be

Effect of forfeiture of privileges.

disponer el gobierno á su arbitrio; pero la compañía La-Sère conservará únicamente como de su propiedad, los edificios que hubiere construido, la parte de camino ya concluida, las locomotoras, trenes y demas objetos empleados en su servicio; y el Gobierno de la República, ó individuo ó compañía á quien este conceda su derecho, lo tendrá para tomarlo todo, previo el pago correspondiente segun el avalúo que al efecto practicarán peritos nombrados por ambas partes.

"Art. 46.—La compañía que forme La-Sère queda obligada á dar al Gobierno general anualmente, los informes que tenga á bien pedirle respecto de la organizacion de la empresa, del estado de los trabajos del ferrocarril, del capital empleado en él, y de todo cuanto el ministerio de fomento crea necesario para tener conocimiento exacto de lo perteneciente á la vía de comunicacion por el Istmo de Tehuantepec.

"Art. 47.—Toda duda ó controversia sobre la inteligencia ó ejecucion de esta ley, será decidida por los tribunales federales competentes de la República mexicana, con arreglo á las leyes de la misma.

"Salon de sesiones del Congreso de la Union.
México, Diciembre 29 de 1868.

JOSÉ M. MATA,
Diputado Presidente.

JUAN SANCHEZ AZCONA,
Diputado Secretario.

JULIO ZÁRATE,
Diputado Secretario.

able to dispose of them at pleasure, but the La Sère Company will only retain as its property the buildings which it may have constructed, the part of the road already finished, the engines, rolling stock and other objects in its service; and the Government of the Republic, or the individual or company to whom it may concede its right, will have to take it all, subject to corresponding reimbursement, according to valuation, which, for the purpose, will be made by arbitrators, named on both sides.

All information concerning the company to be furnished to Government.

ARTICLE 46TH.—The company which La Sère may form, is obliged to furnish to the General Government, annually, the information which may be asked from it, as to the organization of the undertaking, the condition of the works of the railroad, the capital invested in it, and everything that the Minister of the Department of Improvement may desire to ascertain concerning the route of inter-oceanic communication across the Isthmus of Tehuantepec.

Controversies concerning the construction and execution of this law to be decided by Mexican tribunals.

ARTICLE 47TH.—All doubts or controversy as to the construction or execution of this law will be decided by the competent Federal Tribunals of the Republic of Mexico, and in conformity with its laws.

HALL OF THE SESSIONS OF THE CONGRESS OF THE UNION,
MEXICO, 29th December, 1868.

JOSÉ M. MATA,
Deputy President.

JUAN SANCHEZ ASCONA,
Deputy Secretary.

JULIO ZÁRATE,
Deputy Secretary.

"*Por tanto*, mando se imprima, publique, circule y se le dé el debido cumplimiento.

"Dado en el palacio nacional de México, á 2 de Enero de 1869.

BENITO JUAREZ.

"Al C. Blas Balcárcel,
Ministro de Fomento, Colonizacion, Industria y Comercio."

Y lo comunico á vd. para su inteligencia y fines consiguientes.

Independencia y Libertad.
México, Enero 2 de 1869.

BALCÁRCEL."

Therefore, I order that it be printed, published, circulated, and duly observed.

Given in the National Palace of Mexico, on the 2d of January, 1869.

BENITO JUAREZ.

To the citizen Blas Balcárcel,
Minister of Improvement, Colonization, Industry, and Commerce.

And I communicate it to you for your intelligence and corresponding ends.

Independence and Liberty,
Mexico, 2d of Jan'y, 1869.

BALCARCEL.

TRASPASO

DE LA

MODIFICADA CONCESION.

EMILIO LA SERE

A LA

COMPAÑIA DEL FERROCARRIL DE TEHUANTEPEC.

FEBRERO 1° DE 1869.

Sepase por las presentes:

Que el Gobierno de Méjico en Octubre del año de nuetro señor mil, ochocientos, sesenta y siete, concedió autoridad á una compañia que se iba á establecer el Señor Don Emilio La Sère, para que se abriera una comunicacion inter-océanic á traves del Istmo de Tehuantepec, bajo ciertas condiciones y con ciertas privilegios, expresados en la concesion á que se refiere, cuya concesion fué modificada y ratificada por el Congreso de Méjico, el veintinueve de Diciembre del año de nuestro senor, mil ochocientos, sesenta y ocho, y en el dia dos de Enero de mil ochocientos sesenta y nueve fué por el Presidente Constitucional mandada imprimir, publicar, circular y observar y la cual concesion fué en debida forma publicada en el Diario Oficial del Supremo Gobierno de la República de Méjico el dia cuatro de Enero del año de nuestro señor mil, ochocientos, sesenta y nueve.

En tanto que, el dicho La Sère en conformidad con lo concesion ha establecido una compañia con los objetos y con las facultades que quedan mencionados, bajo el título de COMPAÑIA DEL FERROCARRIL DE TEHUANTEPEC, cuya incorporacion fué concedida por la Asamblea General del Estado de Vermont.

CONVEYANCE

OF

AMENDED GRANT.

EMILIO LA SERE

TO THE

TEHUANTEPEC RAILWAY COMPANY.

DATED FEBRUARY 1ST, 1869.

Know all men by these presents:

That whereas the Government of Mexico, in October, one thousand eight hundred and sixty-seven, granted authority to a company to be formed by Don Emilio La Sère to open inter-oceanic communication across the Isthmus of Tehuantepec, upon certain conditions, and with certain rights expressed in the grant, to which reference is to be had, which said grant was modified and confirmed by the Congress of Mexico on the 29th day of December, 1868, and on the 2d day of January, 1869, was ordered by the Constitutional President of Mexico to be printed, published, circulated, and observed, and which was duly printed and published in the Diario Official of the Supreme Government of the Republic of Mexico, on the 4th day of January, 1869; and

Whereas, the said La Sère, in pursuance of the said grant, has formed a company for the purposes and with the powers therein mentioned, under the name of the TEHUANTEPEC RAILWAY COMPANY, the incorporation of which company has been established by the General Assembly of the State of Vermont:

Por lo tanto y en consideracion de la materia de que se trata y de un peso pagado por dicha compañia á dicho La Sère y por otras buenas é importantes consideraciones, dicho Emilio La Sère ha concedido y transferido y por estas presentes concede, y transfere á dicha Compañia del Ferrocarril de Tehuantepec, todos los derechos, privilegios é inmunidades, concedidos, mencionados ó sobreentendidos en la dicha concesion como quedó modificada y ratificada, y por este, el dicho La Sère declara que dicha compañia está revestida con todos los derechos y facultades con que el Gobierno de Méjico intentó revestir la compañia que se iba á formar el dicho La Sère, como queda mencionado en aquella concesion así modificada y ratificada.

En testimonio de lo cual, el dicho La Sère firmó y selló el presente el primer dia de Febrero del año de nuestro señor mil, ochocientos, sesenta y nueve.

EMILIO LA SERE. [SELLO.]

Firmado, sellado y entregado
en presencia de
CHARLES B. ELLIMAN.
J. B. PERRY.

Estados Unidos de la América, Estado de Nueva York, Ciudad y Condado de Nueva York:

Hoy dia diez y ocho de Febrero del año de nuestro senor mil, ochocientos sesenta y nueve, ante mi compareció personalmente Emilio La Sère, á quien doy fé y conozco y en mi presencia firmó el presente declarando haberlo otorgado para los fines y efectos que en él se expresan.

En testimonio de lo cual y para que conste firmo el presente y le sello con el sello de mi oficio el dia y año ántes mencionado.

HENRY STANTON,
Notario Publico,
Estado, Ciudad y Condado de Nueva York.

Therefore, in consideration of the premises, and of one dollar paid by the said company to the said La Sère, and for other good and valuable considerations, the said Emilio La Sère has granted, assigned, and transferred, and does hereby grant, assign, and transfer to the Tehuantepec Railway Company aforesaid all the rights, privileges, and franchises granted, mentioned, or intended in or by the said grant as so modified and confirmed, and does hereby declare that the said company is fully invested with all the rights and powers with which the Government of Mexico intended to clothe the company to be formed by the said La Sère as mentioned in the said grant as so modified and confirmed.

In witness whereof the said La Sère has hereto set his hand and seal, this first day of February, in the year of our Lord one thousand eight hundred and sixty-nine.

EMILIO LA SERE. [SEAL.]

Signed, sealed, and delivered
in presence of
CHARLES B. ELLIMAN.
J. B. PERRY.

United States of America, State of New York, City and County of New York:

On this eighteen'th day of February, in the year of our Lord one thousand eight hundred and sixty-nine, before me personally came Emilio La Sère, to me known to be the individual described in and who executed the foregoing instrument, and acknowledged that he executed the same for the purposes therein mentioned.

In witness whereof I have hereunto set my hand and affixed my official seal, the day and year last above written.

HENRY STANTON,
Notary Public,
State, City, and County of New York.

ACTA

PARA ESTABLECER EL ESCRITURAMIENTO

DE LA

COMPAÑIA DEL FERROCARRIL DE TEHUANTEPEC.

CONSIDERANDO, que el Gobierno de México, en Octubre de mil ocho cientos sesenta y siete, concedió autoridad à una compañia que debia formar Don EMILIO LA SÈRE, para abrir una comunicacion interoceánica al traves del Istmo de Tehuantepec, bajo ciertas condiciones y con ciertos derechos expresados en la concesion hoy archivada en la oficina del Secretario de Estado de este Estado, à la cual es preciso referirse ; y

Considerando, que el citado La Sère, en virtud de dicha concesion y de los artículos de asociacion, há formado una compañia con el objeto y las facultades que en adelante se mencionan, y bajo el nombre de la COMPAÑIA DEL FERROCARRIL DE TEHUANTEPEC, en la forma siguiente, á saber :

ARTICULOS DE ASOCIACION DE LA COMPAÑIA DEL FERROCARRIL DE TEHUANTEPEC.

CONSIDERANDO, que el Gobierno de México, en Octubre de 1867, concedió autoridad á una compañia que debia formar Don Emilio La Sère, para abrir una comunicacion interoceánica al traves del Istmo de Tehuantepec, bajo ciertas condiciones y con ciertos derechos expresados en la concesion á que es preciso referirse ; y

Considerando, que el citado La Sère, en virtud de dicha concesion, há formado una compañia con el objeto y las facultades que aqui se mencionan ;

AN ACT

TO ESTABLISH THE INCORPORATION

OF THE

TEHUANTEPEC RAILWAY COMPANY.

WHEREAS, the Government of Mexico, in October, eighteen hundred and sixty-seven, granted authority to a company to be formed by Don EMILIO LA SÈRE, to open inter-oceanic communication across the Isthmus of Tehuantepec, upon certain conditions and with certain rights expressed in the grant, now on file in the office of the Secretary of State of this State, to which reference is to be had; and

Preamble Mexican grant.

Whereas, the said La Sère, in pursuance of the said grant, has by articles of association formed a company, for the purposes and with the powers hereinafter mentioned, under the name of TEHUANTEPEC RAILWAY COMPANY, in the following words, to wit:

ARTICLES OF ASSOCIATION OF THE TEHUANTEPEC RAILWAY COMPANY, 1867.

WHEREAS, the Government of Mexico, in October, 1867, granted authority to a company to be formed by Don Emilio La Sère to open inter-oceanic communication across the Isthmus of Tehuantepec, upon certain conditions and with certain rights expressed in the grant, to which reference is to be had; and

Articles of association.

Whereas, the said La Sère, in pursuance of the said grant, has formed a company for the purposes and with the powers therein mentioned;

La Sere formed company.

Por tanto, por la presente se atestigua y declara lo que sigue:

Primero.—El nombre de dicha compañia es COMPAÑIA DEL FERROCARRIL DE TEHUANTEPEC.

Segundo.—La compañia continuará mientras dure la citada concesion, y durante el tiempo que se la prorogue.

Tercero.—El capital de la compañia es de diez y ocho millones de pesos, divididos en acciones de cien pesos cada una, cuyo capital será considerado como equivalente de los derechos, privilegios y franquicias otorgados por dicha concesion, y no estará sujeto á otras contribuciones ó demandas, y la cantidad total se dividirá entre los accionistas en la forma siguiente:

A EMILIO LA SÈRE, treinta mil acciones.

A LUIS EUGENIO HARGOUS, mil acciones.

A PEDRO A. HARGOUS, mil acciones.

A HORACIO J. HEISCH, cien acciones.

A SIMON STEVENS, Fideicomisario, ciento cuarenta y siete mil novecientas acciones.

Cuarto.—Los accionistas se reunirán una vez al año, el segundo lúnes de Enero, para elegir directores, hacer ó cambiar los reglamentos, y despachar los demas negocios corrientes de la compañia. Tambien pueden ser convocados en cualquiera otra época por el Presidente ó dos directores cualquiera, avisando con dos meses de anticipacion en anuncio inserto en tres periódicos diarios de la ciudad de Nueva York.

Quinto.—Los accionistas pueden en cualquiera reunion regular, y por los votos de la mayoria de intereses, redactar y establecer reglamentos que provean á la construccion, operacion, y manejo del ferrocarril ú otras obras de la compañia, el modo de admitir nuevos accionistas y el de hacer el traspaso de las acciones y los intereses de los accionistas á nuevos accionistas ó á los apoderados, el número de empleados,

Therefore, it is hereby witnessed and declared as follows:

First.—The name of the said company is The Tehuantepec Railway Company. Name.

Second.—The company is to continue during the continuance of the said grant and of any extension thereof. Duration.

Third.—The capital of the company is eighteen millions of dollars, divided into shares of one hundred dollars each, which capital is to be deemed an equivalent for the rights, privileges, and franchises conferred by the said grant, and not liable to further contribution or assessment; and the whole amount thereof is divided among the shareholders, as follows: Capital, $18,000,000, not liable to assessment.

To Emilio La Sére, thirty thousand shares.
To Louis Eugéne Hargous, one thousand shares.
To Peter A. Hargous, one thousand shares.
To Horace J. Heisch, one hundred shares.
To Simon Stevens, trustee, one hundred and forty-seven thousand nine hundred shares.

Shareholders and distribution of stock.

Fourth.—The shareholders shall meet once a year, on the second Monday of January, to choose the directors, make or change the by-laws, and transact other proper business of the company. They may also be convened at any other time by the President or any two directors, upon two months' previous notice inserted in three of the daily newspapers in the city of New York. Meeting of shareholders and choice of directors.

Fifth.—The shareholders at any regular meeting may, by the votes of a majority in interest, frame and establish by-laws providing for the construction, operation, and management of the railway and other works of the company; the mode of admitting new shareholders, and of transferring the shares and interests of shareholders to new shareholders or assigns; Shareholders may make by-laws.

sus deberes y compensaciones, el modo de celebrar contratos, y generalmente los medios y manera de establecer el ferrocarril y otras obras de la referida compañia, el de proseguirlas, y el de la gerencia y manejo de toda la propriedad y asuntos de dicha compañia.

Sexto.—La compañia no se considerará disuelta por la muerte ó acta de cuaqluier accionista, pero su sucesor en intereses ocupará su lugar, y los derechos de cada accionista dependerán del complimiento, por parte suya, de las obligaciones que se le imponen por la referida concesion, por estos artículos, y por los reglamentos, y en caso de no cumplir con los mismos, despues de habérsele notificado por escrito, y con sesenta dias de anticipacion, que así lo haga, perderá sus derechos, los cuales pasarán á ser adquisicion de los demas accionistas.

Sétimo.—La referida compañia será manejada durante el primer año por cuatro directores, y despues del primer año por siete directores. Para el primer año serán directores, Emilio La-Sère, Luis E. Hargous, y Simon Stevens, que son tres de los actuales accionistas, dejando al Gobierno de México que nombre otro para dicho año. Las tres personas mencionadas conservarán su empleo de directores hasta el segundo Lúnes de Enero de mil ocho cientos sesenta y nueve, y hasta que otros sean elegidos en su lugar. En cada año despues del primero se elegirán anualmente cinco directores por los accionistas y de entre ellos mismos, y los dos restantes serán nombrados por el Gobierno de México.

Octavo.—Toda vacante que ocurra entre los directores, por muerte, dimision, ú otra causa, será cubierta durante el resto del plazo por el voto de los directores restantes.

Noveno.—Los directores de la compañia elegirán uno de entre ellos que será Presidente, y de entre los accionistas se elegirá un Vice-Presidente, un Tesorero, y un Secretario de la compañia.

the number, duties, and compensation of officers; the manner of making contracts, and generally the means and mode of establishing the railway and other works of the said company, and carrying them on, and of controlling and managing all the property and affairs of the said company.

Company not dissolved by death or act of shareholder.

Sixth.—The company shall not be deemed dissolved by the death or act of any shareholder, but his successor in interest shall stand in his place; and the rights of each shareholder shall depend on his own fulfilment of the conditions imposed on him by the said grant, and these articles and the by-laws; and in case of his failure to fulfil the same after sixty days' notice in writing to him to do so, his rights shall be forfeited to and devolve upon the remaining shareholders.

Four directors first year; afterwards seven.

Seventh.—The said company is to be managed during the first year by four directors, and after the first year by seven directors. For the first year Emilio La Sére, Louis E. Hargous, and Simon Stevens, being three of the present shareholders, shall be directors, leaving to the Government of Mexico to appoint one other for that year. The three persons last named shall hold their offices of directors till the second Monday of January, one thousand eight hundred and sixty-nine, and until others are chosen in their places. For every year after the first, five directors shall be chosen annually by the shareholders out of their own number, and the remaining two shall be appointed by the Government of Mexico.

Mexico to have two directors after first year.

Vacancies to be filled by remaining directors.

Eighth.—Any vacancy that may happen among the directors by death, resignation, or otherwise, shall be filled for the remainder of the term by the votes of the remaining directors.

Choice of President, Vice-President, Treasurer, and Secretary.

Ninth.—The directors of the company shall choose one of their number to be President, and from among the stockholders shall choose a Vice-President, a Treasurer, and a Secretary of the company.

Décimo.—Será obligacion del Presidente presidir todas las reuniones de accionistas y directores, y en general atender á los negocios de la compañia bajo la direccion de los accionistas y directores; y en su ausencia ó por imposibilidad de presidir, ocupará su lugar el Vice-Presidente.

Undécimo.—Será obligacion del Tesorero llevar los libros de certificados de acciones, y de todos los fondos de la compañia, que serán depositados en un banco designado por los directores, y serán desembolsados bajo su direccion; pero no se pagará cantidad alguna á no ser en virtud de voto de los directores, y con cheques firmados por el Tesorero y refrendados por el Presidente.

Duodécimo.—Será obligacion del Secretario llevar todos los libros y documentos de la compañia que no sean llevados por el Tesorero, y tomar cuenta y razon de los votos y transacciones de los accionistas y directores.

Décimo-tercio.—El sello será de forma circular, contendrá el escudo de armas de México, con las palabras " COMPAÑIA DEL FERROCARRIL DE TEHUANTEPEC, 1867," grabadas en la circunferencia.

Décimo-cuarto.—Los directores pueden nombrar y relevar á su albedrío todos los empleados subalternos de la compañia, y tendrán el manejo y gerencia general de los negocios de la compañia, siempre con sujecion á la autoridad superior de los accionistas.

Décimo-quinto.—No se incurrirá en ninguna deuda, ó cualquiera otra obligacion por parte de la compañia, á no ser por voto de los directores en reunion regular, y las mismas solo serán pagaderas con las propiedades de la compañia, y en ningun caso estarán sujetos los accionistas á responsabilidades personales de ninguna calse.

Tenth.—It shall be the duty of the President to preside at all meetings of the shareholders and directors, and generally to superintend the business of the company under the direction of the shareholders and directors; in his absence or inability to act, the Vice-President shall take his place.

Duty of President.

Eleventh.—It shall be the duty of the Treasurer to keep the books of share certificates, and all the moneys of the company which shall be deposited in a bank designated by the directors, and shall be disbursed under their direction; but no money shall be paid except in pursuance of a vote of the directors, and upon checks signed by the Treasurer, and countersigned by the President.

Duty of Treasurer.

Twelfth.—It shall be the duty of the Secretary to keep all the books and papers of the company not kept by the Treasurer, and to record the votes and transactions of the shareholders and directors.

Duty of Secretary.

Thirteenth.—The seal shall be in circular form, containing the coat of arms of Mexico, with the words "Tehuantepec Railway Company, 1867," on the circumference.

Description of seal.

Fourteenth.—The directors may appoint and remove at pleasure all subordinate officers of the company, and shall have the general management and control of the affairs of the company, subject always to the superior authority of the shareholders.

Control of company in directors subject to authority of shareholders.

Fifteenth.—No debt or other obligation of the company can be incurred except by a vote of the directors at a regular meeting, and the same must be made payable only out of the property of the company; and in no event shall the shareholders be subject to any personal responsibility whatever.

Contraction of debt. No individual liabilities.

Décimo-sexto.—Todo contrato de la compañia debe ser firmado por el Presidente y el Secretario, y sellado con el sello de la compañia.

En fé de lo cual, el citado Emilio La-Sère y los demas accionistas de dicha compañia, han firmado y sellado la presente, hoy, diez y seis de Diciembre de mil ocho cientos sesenta y siete.

EMILIO LA-SÉRE. [SELLO.]
L. E. HARGOUS. [SELLO.]
P. A. HARGOUS. [SELLO.]
H. J. HEISCH. [SELLO.]
SIMON STEVENS, [SELLO.]
Fideicomisario.

Sellado y entregado en
presencia de
CHARLES B. ELLIMAN.
W. H. MORGAN.

Por tanto,

La Asamblea General del Estado de Vermont decreta por la presente:

Artículo 1.—Que Emilio La-Sère, Luis Eugenio Hargous, Pedro A. Hargous, Horacio J. Heisch, y Simon Stevens, y cualesquiera otras personas que en lo sucesivo sean accionistas de dicha compañia, quedan autorizadas por la presente en cuerpo corporado bajo el nombre de Compañia del Ferrocarril de Tehuantepec, con todos los derechos, privilegios y franquicias otorgadas por la antedicha concesion del Gobierno de México, ó que en lo sucesivo sean otorgadas por cualquiera concesion adicional, con el fin de llevar á cabo todos los objetos á que se refiere dicha concesion, con sujecion á las cláusulas de los antedichos artículos de asociacion,

Sixteenth.—Every contract of the company must be signed by the President and Secretary, and sealed with the seal of the company.

Contracts to be signed by President and Secretary and sealed.

In witness whereof the said Emilio La Sére and the other shareholders of the said company have hereto set their hands and seals, this sixteenth day of December, one thousand eight hundred and sixty-seven.

EMILIO LA SÉRE. [SEAL.]
L. E. HARGOUS. [SEAL.]
P. A. HARGOUS. [SEAL.]
H. J. HEISCH. [SEAL.]
SIMON STEVENS, [SEAL.]
Trustee.

Sealed and delivered in
the presence of
CHARLES B. ELLIMAN.
W. H. MORGAN.

Therefore,

It is hereby enacted by the General Assembly of the State of Vermont:

Section 1.—That Emilio La Sére, Louis Eugéne Hargous, Peter A. Hargous, Horace J. Heisch, and Simon Stevens, and such other persons as shall hereafter become stockholders in said company, are hereby constituted a body corporate by the name of the TEHUANTEPEC RAILWAY COMPANY, with all the rights, privileges, and franchises given by the above-mentioned grant from the Government of Mexico, or that may hereafter be given by any amendment or enlargement of said grant, or by any additional grant, and for the purpose of carrying out all the objects contemplated in said grant, subject to the provisions of the aforesaid articles of association.

Incorporation of Tehuantepec Railway Company.

Artículo 2.—Y la referida compañia queda autorizada para construir, comprar ó fletar buques de vapor ó de otra clase, y todo el equipo necesario para los mismos, y para hacerlos navegar desde y hasta cualquiera de los términos del citado Ferrocarril de Tehuantepec, á cualquiera otro puerto ó puertos, con objeto de trasportar flete ó pasageros desde y hasta cualquiera de dichos términos; y puede adquirir y conservar los bienes raices necesarios para establecer convenientes diques, atracaderos, muelles y almacenes para los mismos.

Artículo 3.—Esta acta tendrá efecto desde su aprobacion.

Aprobado el 10 de Noviembre de 1868.

JOHN B. PAGE,
Gobernador.

ESTADO DE VERMONT,
OFICINA DEL SECRETARIO DE ESTADO.

Certifico que lo que antecede es copia exacta del acta de la Asamblea General, aprobada el 10 de Noviembre, 1868, y archivada en esta oficina.

[L. S.] En fé de lo cual firmo con mi nombre, y estampo el sello de esta oficiana, en Montpelier, á once de Noviembre del año del Señor mil ocho-cientos sesenta y ocho.

GEORGE NICHOLS,
Secretario de Estado.

Section 2.—And the said company is authorized to build, purchase, or charter steam or other vessels, and all proper equipments for the same, and to run the same to and from either of the termini of said Tehuantepec Railway to any other port or ports, for the purpose of carrying freight or passengers to and from the same; and may acquire and hold any real estate necessary for suitable docks, piers, wharves, and warehouses for the same.

Authority to build or charter vessels and hold real estate.

Section 3.—This act shall take effect from its passage.

Act to take effect immediately.

Approved, Nov. 10, 1868.

JOHN B. PAGE,
Governor.

STATE OF VERMONT,
OFFICE OF SECRETARY OF STATE.

I hereby certify that the foregoing is a true copy of an act of the General Assembly, approved November 10, 1868, and now on file in this office.

In witness whereof, I hereunto subscribe my name, and cause the seal of this office to be affixed, at Montpelier, this eleventh day of November, A. D. one thousand eight hundred and sixty-eight.

[L. S.]

GEORGE NICHOLS,
Secretary of State.

PROJECT

ADOPTED BY THE

TEHUANTEPEC RAILWAY COMPANY,

FOR THE CONSTRUCTION OF THE PROPOSED

RAILWAY, CARRIAGE-ROAD AND TELEGRAPH LINE,

ACROSS THE ISTHMUS OF TEHUANTEPEC,

AUGUST 31ST, 1868.

Approved by the Mexican Government, January 5th, 1869.

ENGINEER'S OFFICE,
NEW YORK, August, 1868.

To SIMON STEVENS, ESQ.,
President of the Tehuantepec
Railway Company, New York.

SIR: In accordance with your instructions, I herewith submit the general specifications of the project for the contemplated line of communication by railroad between the Gulf of Mexico and the Pacific Ocean, across the Isthmus of Tehuantepec, based upon the detailed information in your possession, acquired by the various surveys and explorations which have been made from time to time, and which I have carefully studied, having in view as a guide the spirit and letter of the grant conferred by President Juarez, of the Mexican Republic, upon Don Emilio La Sere, and under which grant your Company is organized.

Accompanying the specification is a Map, exhibiting in *red* line the proposed route of Railroad across the Isthmus of Tehuantepec, and in *green* the route for a Carriage Road, and *dotted in yellow* the line of Telegraph.

With the data in my possession, I have selected these lines of route as in my judgment best calculated to further the interests of both parties in the grant, having always in view the true interests of the Company and the wants of commerce.

The surveys of the Goatzacoalcos River show ample depth of water from the bar at the mouth of the river to Minatitlan, a distance of twenty miles.

It would appear that the bar has undergone little if any change since the time of Cortez; and the nature of the ridge constituting the bar offers no serious impediment to modern skill in opening a channel of three hundred feet in width through the bar, with a depth of water at low tide of eighteen feet. After the bar is passed, sea steamers will find no difficulty in making Minatitlan at all stages of water; and for sailing vessels, the advantages of this terminus may repay the outlay requisite to provide steam tugs for the ascent of the river to Minatitlan. Though future examinations may show the possibility of the existence of a feasible line for a railroad from the mouth of the river, and following the line of sand hills towards Miniapan, and crossing the Rio Tierra Nueva, and thence following the ridge to near the village of Cosuliacaque, where it would branch from the route which makes Minatitlan its terminus, yet it would not be prudent at this date to fix upon the precise northern terminus of the road on the Gulf, as before determining so important a question minute and detailed examinations should be made, more than such as would suffice for the determination of the bare *feasibility* of routes.

The principles which should govern in the construction of the road would be the same in either case.

The same may be said in reference to the terminus on the Pacific coast. Ventosa has been regarded as the proper terminus, and I propose for descriptive purposes so to regard it; yet I would suggest that, if possible, the right be reserved of making Salina Cruz the port for the terminus of the road, should future examinatlons show its advantages over the port of Ventosa. As the proper crossing of the Tehuantepec River is at Huilotepec in either case, it affects neither the location nor length of the road to any appreciable extent.

It should be borne in mind that even in the United States, comparatively well settled and open, changes of location are frequently considered desirable *after* the construction of the roads have made some progress: how much more will this possibly be called for in a country so difficult and heavily timbered as this, and where in the absence of correct maps the precise bearing of important and controlling obstacles cannot be known with certainty until minute examination has developed them. Experience has shown that of all the funds invested in public works, none makes a better return than that expended in determining beyond question the most advantageous locations.

Having in view these possible modifications, the general line of location of the works and the principles which will govern in their construction may be stated as follows:

I.—LOCATION OF ROAD.

Leaving the precise point in the village of Minatitlan open to future negotiation with property-holders, the line taking the slope of the ridge north of that village, passes just south of Cosuliacaque, thence just south of Tesistepec, following (with but slight variation and for the purpose of correct alignment) the line of overflow, thence curving to the south and east of Lake Otiapa, thence curving southerly to the eastward of the hacienda of Almagro, thence nearly straight to within one mile west of Mount Encantada, thence curving westwardly, and direct to the selected crossing of the Jaltepec, about 5 miles west of Suchil, known as "Hargousana."

For this division of the road, the line is quite direct, the curves of easy radius, and the grades gentle. The principle governing in its location being to preserve the grade from about 3 to 5 feet above the level of extreme overflow, and at the foot of the slopes of high land which constitutes the dividing ridge between the waters of the San Juan and Goatzacoalcos Rivers, and following this line to preserve the shortest practicable route to the crossing of the Jaltepec. At Hargousana the Jaltepec is crossed at a level of 110 feet above high tide at Ventosa; the line from thence south, following a depression in the ridge, and rising for 1½ miles at the rate of 60 feet to the mile, to the summit which divides the waters of the Jaltepec from those of the Jumuapa River. This summit is just south of the Picadura to Suchil, and is 290 feet above the tide.* The line thence descends for 8 miles, crossing several branches of the Jumuapa, until it reaches the latter at Paso de la Puerta; crossing the river at this place at a height of 155 feet above tide, the line then follows a branch of the Jumuapa which lies in the direction of the route to the summit between the valleys of the Jumuapa and the Sarabia, a distance of 6 miles, 2 miles of which is at the rate of 60 feet to the mile, with a total rise in that distance of 195 feet. From this summit the line continues direct to the Sarabia River, a distance of 4 miles, over a gently

---

* Where reference is made to tide, it means the level of high tide at Ventosa.

undulating profile, and crossing the latter river at a height above tide of 305 feet (or a fall of but 47 feet in 4 miles), curves to the eastward, and following a branch of the Sarabia for 2 miles, with a rise of 20 feet per mile, reaches the summit between the Sarabia and Malatengo Rivers at a height above tide of 340 feet; thence following over a gently descending grade a tributary of the Malatengo (Arroyo de los Venados about 2 miles south of Boca del Monte), it crosses the latter river about 280 feet above tide, and near its junction with the Rio Almaloya, and skirting the base of the upland between the two rivers, takes the valley of the Rio Almaloya, which it follows to the plains of Chivela, a distance of 24 miles, rising in that distance 410 feet, or a mean rise of 17 feet per mile, with no grade of over 25 feet per mile. Still following a branch of the Almaloya (the Otate), it crosses the Chivela plains, and enters the pass of Masahua, at a height of 793 feet above tide, or a rise of 103 feet in 4½ miles. This is the extreme height of the grade at the summit pass which divides the waters which flow into the Pacific from those which flow into the Atlantic.

At this point, within a hundred yards of the head waters of the Almaloya, a branch of the Rio Verde (Torrente de Masahua), heads up between Cerro Espinosa and Cerro Masahuita of the Masahua range, and offers a means of gradual descent to the Pacific plains.

Following the circuitous valley of this stream a distance of 9 miles, and descending at the rate of 60 feet per mile for 8 miles, we reach the foot of the mountain range, and crossing the Rio Verde at the Rancho de la Martar, at a height of 240 feet above tide, find ourselves on the Pacific plains. From this point to whichever port in the Pacific is selected, the most direct line is through Huilotepec, where a good crossing of the Tehuantepec River offers. The total distance from Minatitlan to Ventosa by this location is 162 miles. It might be thought that Tehuantepec, where the crossing of the river of that name offers some advantages, should be included in the line of the location; but in a great international road, as this is designed to be, it is scarcely proper to add 4 miles of distance to the main line of road for any purpose of local advantage, however desirable it might be.

II.—CARRIAGE ROAD.

The Carriage Road, which it is in contemplation to complete previous to the construction of the railroad, will serve not more as an auxiliary to the latter than as a means of developing the resources of the Isthmus, and will, to avail as much as possible of the large expenditure already made to this end, be located as follows:—From Minatitlan to Cosuliacaque, thence to Jaltipan, thence to Acayucam, thence to Sayula, thence passing 1½ miles west of the Hacienda of Almegro, thence to Pavons Monterea, thence to Hargousana (Jaltepec River), thence to Tortugas, thence to Sarabia, thence to Antigua Hacienda, thence to Almaloya and Otate, thence to Chivela, thence to the Rio Verde, thence to San Geronimo, thence to Tehuantepec, thence to Ventosa—a distance of 208 miles. The road bed to be cleared and ditched where necessary, culverts to be built at the stream crossings, and the Jaltepec, Tortugas, Puerta, Sarabia, Malatengo, Arroyo de Xochiapa, Almaloya, Torente de Guichilona, Rio de los Perros, Tehuantepec Rivers to be bridged with substantial timber truss bridges on pile bent abutments and piers.

The timber to be cleared for a width of 50 feet, and the road-bed to be properly graded for wheel travel for a width of at least 15 feet. The best assurance of the proper character of this portion of the work will rest in the fact that the economy with which the railroad construction will progress will be largely dependent upon the efficiency of this road, and its ability to sustain the heavy traffic of material and supplies which will seek it at all times and seasons. It will be perceived that the railroad takes the valley of the Almaloya, while the carriage road follows the picaduras near and to west of Nisi Conejo, distant from the railroad line some five miles. This grows out of the fact that the valley of the Almaloya offers no inducement for settlement; and if the carriage-line were taken through it at great expense, it would be merely for the use of laborers and supplies, and would go into disuse on the completion of the railroad; whereas, as now located, the carriage road would be of value to the material interests of the Isthmus as now opened and in prospect, and serve passably well by picaduras to the railroad line, for the supply to the latter of provisions and material during its construction.

III.—GRADUATION, MASONRY, AND BRIDGING.

Wherever the banks are less than 8 feet in height, the site of the road will be cleared to a width of 100 feet, and all perishable matter burnt up; where the embankment is higher, the land will be cleared for a distance of 15 feet from the foot of the slopes. Wherever the embankments are less than 3 feet in height, the ground will be cleared of all perishable matter, the stumps of the trees will be grubbed up, and all muck and vegetable matter removed. In excavating through heavy timber, the latter will be cleared at least 50 feet from the top of the slopes.

The width of all embankments at grade of a height of 25 feet and under, will be 16 feet, for a single track road, with side slopes of 1½ to 1. Embankments of over 25 feet in height will, for every 10 feet in height, have an additional width at grade of 1 foot. The excavation in earth will be 26 feet wide at grade level, with ditches of 4 feet in width on each side, and 1½ feet in depth, and a side slope of 1½ to 1. Side cuts will have a width of grade of 20 feet, with ditches of 4 feet in width. Rock excavation will be 22 feet in width, with side slopes of ¼ to ⅕, depending upon the nature of the rock, with ditches of 3 feet in width. Wherever the excavation exceeds the quantity requisite to make the bank, the surplus shall be used to widen the bank to 30 feet for a double track; and on the contrary, wherever there is a deficiency in the cut to make the adjoining bank, the quantity needed shall be obtained by widening the cut uniformly, provided in so doing rock excavation be not encountered.

There will be no grade over 60 feet per mile, and no curves of less than 1,100 feet radius. There are many first-class roads in the United States with a ruling grade greater than this, and with curves of less radius. A speed of 20 miles per hour can be maintained on such grade, with a train of over 500 passengers and their baggage. Such grade, therefore, cannot be considered objectionable for the Isthmus transit.

MASONRY AND BRIDGING.

Ths masonry of all bridges or culverts, where they do not rest on the solid rock, shall in all cases be founded on hard bottom below the scouring action of the stream. Wherever a hard bottom cannot be had, the foundations shall rest on a grillage of timber, at such depths as shall insure their being constantly wet. The timber shall be of large dimensions, leveled on a uniform bearing, and placed in contact side by side; and hewn on the four faces, and covered with a platform of 6-inch plank, well bolted and spiked to the same. Where soft bottom or quicksand is encountered, the whole area shall be properly piled to a good bearing, the piles capped, and the spaces filled in with broken stone, and floored and spiked or bolted to the caps. The masonry of culverts shall be good picked rubble masonry—heavy stones selected for the lower courses—which shall be properly bonded, breaking joint throughout, and conforming in every particular to detailed plans, which will be furnished by the engineer for each work.

All walls which come to grade, or parapet walls, shall be neatly coped with flat stone of good dimensions, well and truly squared and bedded. The arch stones shall in all cases be the whole depth of the arch, cut on the ends or rings, and the whole shall in every respect be what is known in the United States as "first class culvert masonry," and laid dry.

Abutment and pier masonry for bridges shall be substantial, durable stone, of as large dimensions as can be readily procured, laid in courses, with cut beds and square joints, properly bonded and breaking joint; A proper proportion of headers, which shall extend *into* the backing, and binding it to the face work. No stone shall be less than one foot in thickness for heavy work, and no stone shall have a less bed than twice its rise. The coping for such work shall be of large dimensions, neatly cut, and properly cramped and doweled, the whole well laid in full beds of good cement mortar, agreeably to the plans of the engineer, which shall be in detail for each work. The foundations will be as previously specified, and laid with extreme care —the work of the description known in the United States as "cut range work, rock face."

BRIDGING.

All the permanent truss bridges of over 50 feet span will be of *Iron*. The trusses, where the level of the water will admit of it, to be so placed that the track shall be on their upper chords. The plans of these bridges will be matured by the engineer in conformity with the best practice of the day, and made under his directions, in the United States, and taken out in pieces, and put up in conformity with his directions. The shorter bridges, and trestles over ravines, and approaches to permanent bridges, and other places where, for facilitating the completion of the work, rapidity of execution is of importance, timber structures will be used until after the opening of the road, when they will be replaced either by solid banks, arched masonry, or iron bridging, as may be most to the interest of the Company. These structures will be carefully planned, of heavy, durable timber, and well put together with iron bolts, and in a workmanlike manner, agreeable to the method adopted on first class roads in the United States.

IV.—TUNNELS.

The tunnels which may be needed will be of a full size for a single track road, that is to say, of a clear width of 18 feet, and a height of 19 feet above rails. In the event of the rock or other material encountered in the excavation of the tunnel proving treacherous, or liable to failure, the same will be properly arched with brick, leaving the dimensions in the clear of the tunnel as above stated.

V.—GAUGE AND RAIL.

Omitting in this place the arguments and discussions upon which the decision is based, it will be sufficient to state that the experience of many years use of various gauges in the United States has demonstrated the fact that, neither in net tonnage transported, nor in speed or safety or economy, have the wider gauges established any superiority over the narrower gauge of 4 feet 8½ inches, whilst in a new enterprise, especially, it has manifest disadvantages. Accordingly, it is proposed to adopt the prevailing gauge in use in the United States, viz., of 4 feet 8½ inches. The dimensions and weight of rail proposed is that of the pattern of the Erie Railroad and the Union Pacific, with the iron fish-joints now being introduced on the former road as the latest modern practice, using therewith the superior quality of cross-ties found on the Isthmus, to the number of 3,000 to each mile of track, with *four* 6-inch wrought iron spikes to each cross-tie.

VI.—TURNOUTS.

At Minatitlan, and at the port on the Pacific, the road will be opened with *four* tracks in addition to the main track, giving a total of over 10,000 lineal feet of turnout at each of these points. At Hargousana, or at the point selected for the repair shops of the Company, there will be at the least 10,000 feet of side track, and, in addition, there will be 8 intermediate stations with 2,000 feet of side track at each, or a total of nearly 9 miles of side track; to be increased at such points, and to such extent, from time to time, as the wants of the road may indicate as desirable.

VII.—DEPOTS AND FIXTURES.

There will be a central engine house and repair-shop at "Hargousana," or such other point as may be selected, with stalls for 10 engines, with arrangements for ultimate extension, to be built of brick, with slate or iron roof, and turn-tables of iron. The locomotive repair shops, with steam engine, machinery, and tools for repairs of all the engines in use, and so planned as to admit of extension for ultimate use in the construction of cars and carriages, to be of brick, with iron roof; substantial houses to be erected for the use of the mechanics and their families.

At each terminal station there will be an engine-house, with stalls for 6 engines, also of brick, with iron roof, and repair shop, with the requisite tools for smaller repairs, and turn-tables of iron. The passenger houses at these terminal stations, and also at the central station, to be substantial structures of brick with iron roofs. Refreshment rooms and other accommodations, similar to the first class station houses in the United States, to be provided at these points. The freight houses at these terminal stations to be of iron, of single story, at least 300 feet in length, 30 feet in width, with derricks, cranes and scales, and side tracks for the prompt disposal of freight. The freight houses at the intermediate stations to be of timber, about 90 feet by 30 feet, closed in securely from the weather, with rooms under the same roof for passengers and officers of the Company; at each of the stations and at intermediate points, giving a supply for every 10 miles of road, iron water tanks will be provided, each to hold at least 6,000 gallons of water, with the most approved iron pumps (wherever the latter are needed) and fixtures complete, and timber wood sheds, each of a capacity of from 300 to 400 cords of wood.

VIII.—RIVER NAVIGATION.

The channel through the bar at the mouth of the Goatzacoalcos to be excavated to a width of 300 feet, and depth of 18 feet at low water. The river from Minatitlan to Suchil, and Jaltepec to Hargousana, to be cleared of snags, and dredged where necessary to a depth of 2½ feet at extreme low water; dangerous rocks to be removed, and the river rendered safe for light-draught steamers to those points.

IX.—PIERS AND WHARFS.

The only work of a temporary character which is contemplated, will be that of the piers and wharfs, the proper extent of which cannot be determined until a better knowledge of the localities shall furnish the requisite information to govern their construction.

At Ventosa, for convenience of landing at all times, a breakwater will be built from within the Morro point, curving towards the southeast for a length of about 1,500 feet into 30 feet of water.

This pier will be 40 feet wide at top, and with a side slope of 3 inches to a foot, and built of cribs of timber, sunk and filled with stone, the sides planked with 6-inch plank, bolted and spiked to the crib timbers.

The pier will be 10 feet above high water, and will form a nucleus for further and more permanent works as may be needed.

A double rail track will extend to the head of the pier.

At Minatitlan, a bulk-head, with a frontage of at least 600 feet, will be built of crib work filled in with stone, to be replaced ultimately by iron sheet piling if necessary.

A double line of rails to run parallel to the front. The wharfs at Suchil and Hargousana will be formed by piling the requisite frontage on the river, and with caps bolted to the pile heads, with heavy plank flooring spiked to the caps, the whole properly braced and bolted.

X.—LIGHT HOUSES.

A brick or iron tower, of such height as, together with its site, will give an elevation of 130 feet above the sea, will be built on the west bank of the Goatzacoalcos River, and furnished with a sea light capable of being seen at sea for a distance of 20 miles.

A beacon or harbor light will be placed in about 8 feet water, within the bar, on an iron screw-pile pier, elevated 15 feet above high water.

A similar light, of the same order and elevation, to be placed on the Morro point, and a beacon light on the pier head, will be put up at Ventosa.

XI.—TELEGRAPH.

The telegraph line will commence at the mouth of the Goatzacoalcos River, and following the sand hills, cross the Rio Tierra Nueva near the Rancho Calcados, and, taking the high land above the overflow, reach Minatitlan; thence it will follow the carriage road until after the completion of the railroad, when it will be transferred permanently to the latter line. A branch also will extend from Hargousana to Suchil.

The above specification embraces what would be considered in the United States that of a first class road, with a capacity sufficient for the immediate transportation, without the possibility of hindrance or delay, of a yearly tonnage of 100,000 tons of merchandise and 100,000 passengers.

In conclusion, I would beg leave to recommend that in view of the rapid improvements now being made in all branches of mechanical work, particularly such as the one under consideration, the engineer should not be confined too closely to existing works elsewhere as a guide, but may, with the approval of the Company, as the work progresses, introduce such improvements as may be thought conducive to the success of the enterprise, although not specified in the above project.

JULIUS W. ADAMS, *Engineer.*

Vice-President of the American Society of Civil Engineers.

Examined, approved and recommended for adoption,

(Signed,) MARSHALL O. ROBERTS.

Adopted by the TEHUANTEPEC RAILWAY COMPANY, New York, August 31st, 1868.

(Signed,) SIMON STEVENS,

[SEAL.] *President.*

Tehuantepec Railway Co.

Attest:

(Signed,) PETER A. HARGOUS,

Secretary.

ESTIMATED COST OF RAILWAY.

ENGINEER'S OFFICE,
TEHUANTEPEC RAILWAY CO.,
NEW YORK, Feb. 22d, 1869.

SIMON STEVENS, ESQ.,
President.

SIR: At your request I have examined all the maps, profiles, and reports, and such other data in my possession bearing in any way upon the subject of the cost of constructing a railway across the Isthmus of Tehuantepec, and beg leave to report the result as follows:

I have taken the quantities of material, as estimated by Major Barnard in 1852 for the construction of the several divisions of this road, and make such changes in the prices, as in my judgment were called for to represent the comparative values of executing the various kinds of works then and now.

I have adopted 4 feet 8 inches as the guage of the road, being all that is needed for requisite power to move anything which can be transported to advantage on railroads. I have assumed 16 feet width of banks, and 26 feet width of cuts in earth as sufficient, and should recommend that most of the bridges of any extent, as well as embankments over 20 feet in height, should be built on trestles to serve until the road is opened, when the more permanent structure can be put in.

ESTIMATE.

Wagon road from Minatitlan *via* Jaltepec crossing at Hargousana to Ventosa, complete, 208 miles......	$160,000
Passenger and freight house at Hargousana or Jaltepec crossing, including machine shop, fixtures and machinery for the whole road......	120,000

Passenger and freight houses and light repair shops at Ventosa and Minatitlan...	120,000
Wood and water stations...............	18,000
Clearing, grading, bridging, and preparation of roadbed complete, from Minatitlan to Ventosa, 162 miles..............	5,948,000
For one mile of superstructure I estimate as follows. (Iron imported free of duty).	8,500
172 miles of track including 10 miles of turnouts complete....................	1,462,000

EQUIPMENT.

8 freight engines, 30 tons, each	$14,000..	$112,000
6 passenger " 26 " "	12,000..	72,000
14 " cars...............	4,000..	56,000
10 " and baggage, 2d class	3,500..	35,000
120 freight cars, open and box....	900..	108,000
35 repair cars of all kinds........		12,000

This equipment will suffice to open the road with a capacity for 100,000 passengers, and 100,000 tons of freight yearly: Of course this item will undergo a constant and steady increase to meet the requirements of the trade.

Recapitulation of cost of opening passenger and freight traffic from the Gulf of Mexico to the Pacific Ocean.

Auxiliary wagon road, Minatitlan to Ventosa..............................	$160,000
Railroad fixtures at Jaltepec, Ventosa, Minatitlan, and line of R. R...........	258,000
Grading, bridging, and preparation of roadbed, Minatitlan to Ventosa, 162 miles.	5,948,000
Superstructure, 172 miles...............	1,462,000
Engineering and superintendence........	600,000
Equipments	395,000
	$8,823,000

Jaltepec or Hargousana becomes a proper point for the great machine shops of the company; although not in the centre of the road when complete, it is within the ordinary days run of an engine to Ventosa, and the river from Minatitlan will always be used more or less as far as this point, and, if the enterprise is destined to work any permanent benefit to the Isthmus, it must be looked for through the building up of a trading centre, accessible in all directions by the limited means at command of the natives. Such a point is the neighborhood of Suchil, and the establishment of the machine shops of the company at this point, will inure to the mutual benefit of the road, and the local traffic which no other point could promise.

The passage from Minatitlan by train to Ventosa may be estimated at eight hours.

It is a difficult matter to estimate the progressive increase in travel growing out of increased facilities for its accommodation.

It is not likely that the travel the first year would form any standard of comparison for what would inevitably follow. All great improvments, even when projected on established lines of travel, shows this.

If the advantages of a far more healthy and salubrious climate, a saving of 1,700 miles of sea voyage, commodious harbors on either side, increased economy of transportation, freedom from taxation, and the enormous impulse which the development of the China trade will give to the shorter routes of travel across the continent, fail to give your road an income equal at least to that of the Panama railroad, the result will falsify all the predictions which are legitimately deducible from the experience of existing lines of travel.

Respectfully submitted,

JULIUS W. ADAMS,

Engineer.

Bond of the Tehuantepec Railway Co. given to the Republic of Mexico, pursuant to Article 16*th of the grant.*

BOND.

Know all men by these presents :

That we, the Tehuantepec Railway Company as principal, and Marshall O. Roberts as surety, are jointly and severally held and firmly bound unto the Republic of Mexico in the penal sum of one hundred thousand dollars [100,000] of the coined money of Mexico, to be paid to the said Republic at the National Treasury in the city of Mexico; to which payment well and truly to be made, we bind ourselves, our successors, and representatives firmly by these presents.

Sealed with our seals, and dated the eighteenth day of February, in the year of our Lord one thousand eight hundred and sixty-nine.

Whereas, the Government of Mexico, on the sixth day of October, A. D., one thousand eight hundred and sixty-seven, granted authority to a company to be formed by Don Emilio La Sère to open interoceanic communication across the Isthmus of Tehuantepec, upon certain conditions and with certain rights expressed in the grant to which reference is to be had, which grant was modified and confirmed by the Congress of Mexico, the 29th day of December, 1868, and on the 2d day of January, 1869, was ordered by the Constitutional President of Mexico to be printed, published, circulated, and observed, and which was duly printed and published in the Diario Official of the Supreme Government of the Republic of Mexico, on the 4th day of January, 1869, and,

Whereas, the said La Sère, in pursuance of the said grant, has formed a company which has procured from the General Assembly of the State of Vermont the establishment of its incorporation, which company is established and organized in such manner as to fulfil all the requirements of the said grant.

Now then, the condition of this obligation is such, that if the company shall, within eighteen months from the 2d day of January, 1869, as specified in the said grant, comply with its obligations to present plans and to commence and finish the construction of the roads and telegraph line mentioned in the said grant, and according to the terms thereof, and if the said company shall, within the said specified periods, comply with its obligations as mentioned in Article sixteen of the said grant, and according to the terms thereof, then this obligation shall be void, otherwise it shall continue in full force.

(Signed) SIMON STEVENS,
[SEAL.] *President Tehuantepec Railway Co.*

(Signed) MARSHALL O. ROBERTS.
Surety.

(Signed) P. A. HARGOUS,
Secretary.

UNITED STATES OF AMERICA.

STATE, CITY AND COUNTY OF NEW YORK.

On the eighteenth day of February, A. D., one thousand eight hundred and sixty-nine, before me, Henry Stanton, a notary public, duly commissioned and sworn in and for the city and county of New York, personally came Peter A. Hargous, to me known to be the Secretary of the Tehuantepec Railway Company, with whom I am personally acquainted, who, being by me duly sworn, said that he resided in the city and county of New York, in the State of New York, in the United States of America; that he was Secretary of the said Tehuantepec Railway Company; that he knew the common seal of the said company;

that the seal affixed to the foregoing instrument was such common seal; that it was so affixed by order of the Board of Directors of the said company, and that he signed his name thereto by the like order as Secretary of the said company:

And the said Peter A. Hargous further said, that he was acquainted with Simon Stevens, and knew him to be the President of said company; that the signature of the said Simon Stevens subscribed to the said instrument was in the genuine handwriting of the said Simon Stevens, and was thereto subscribed by the like order of the said Board of Directors, and in the presence of him, the said Peter A. Hargous.

And, also, on the day and year aforesaid, before me personally, came Simon Stevens, to me known to be the President of the Tehuantepec Railway Company, with whom I am personally acquainted, who, being by me duly sworn, said that he resided in the city and county of New York, in the State of New York, in the United States of America; that he was President of the said Tehuantepec Railway Company; that he knew the common seal of the said company; that the seal affixed to the foregoing instrument was such common seal; that it was so affixed by order of the Board of Directors of the said company, and he signed his name thereto by the like order as President of the said company.

And, also, on the day and year aforesaid, personally came Marshall O. Roberts, to me known to be one of the individuals described in and who executed the foregoing instrument as surety, and acknowledged that he executed the same as and for the purposes therein mentioned.

In witness whereof, I have hereunto set my hand and affixed my official seal the day and year
[SEAL.] last above written.

HENRY STANTON,
Notary Public in and for the City and County of New York.

El Consul general de la Republica Mejicana en los Estados Unidos.

Certifico que la firma y sello que anteceden y dicen Henry Stanton, son del Escribano publico, del mismo nombre y los mismos que acostumbra usar en todos los documentos que autoriza, por lo que se les debe dar entera fé y crédito. En fé de lo cual doy la presente en la Ciudad de Nueva York à dos de Marzo, de mil ochocientos sesenta y uneve.

(Signed) JUAN N. NAVARRO.

[L. S.]

Certifico tambien que la fianza anterior suscrita por Mr. Marshall O. Roberts, me ha sido presentado hoy por la Compañia del Ferrocarril de Tehuantepec, para cumplir con el Art 16 de la Concession, por no haber actualmente en Washington representante alguno del Gob°. Mejicano, y que yo he hecho presente á dicha Compa. que aunque creo la fianza enteramente satisfactoria, no tengo instrucciones para recibirla, y la remitiré por el próximo vapor à mi Gob°. para que la examine y diga si está ó no conforme con ella.

(Signed) JUAN N. NAVARRO.

[L. S.]

Certifico tambien que el documente anterior es una copia perfectamente exacta del original que envio à mi Gobierno para su exámen.

(Signed) JUAN N. NAVARRO.

[L. S.]

NUEVA YORK, Marzo 29, de 1869.

NUEVA YORK, Abril 14 de, 1869.

Habiendo recibido hoy instrucciones y autorizacion de mi Gobierno para aprobar la fianza anterior, caso de encontrarla satisfactoria, y siendo tal en mi concepto por la presente y en nombre del Supremo Gobierno de la Republica Mejicana, admito la dicha fianza y declaro que la Compañia ha cumplido plenamente con las obligaciones que le impone el articulo 16 de la concesion aprobada por el Congreso de la Union el 29 de Diciembre de 1868, y sancionada por el ejecutivo el 2 de Enero de 1869.

(Signed) JUAN N. NAVARRO.

SEAL.]

[TRANSLATION.]

The Consul General of the Republic of Mexico in the United States.

I certify that the preceding signature and seal saying "Henry Stanton," are those of the Notary Public of that name, and the same that he affixes to all the documents that he authenticates, and are, therefore, entitled to all faith and credit.

In witness whereof, I give the present in the City of New York on the 2d day of March, 1869.

[L. S.] (Signed) JOHN N. NAVARRO.

I also certify, that the preceding bond, signed by Marshall O. Roberts, has been presented to me to-day by the Tehuantepec Railway Company, in order to comply with the 16th Article of the grant, because there is not actually, in Washington, any representative of the Mexican Government; and I have made known to said company, that although I consider the bond to be entirely satisfactory, I have no instructions to receive it, but will forward it by the first steamer to my Government, in order that they may examine it and state whether it is satisfactory or not.

[L. S.] (Signed) JOHN N. NAVARRO.

I also certify, that the foregoing document is a copy perfectly exact of the original that I send to my Government for its examination.

[L. S.] (Signed) JOHN N. NAVARRO.

NEW YORK, March 29, 1869.

NEW YORK, April 14th, 1869.

Having received to-day, instructions and authority from my Government to approve the foregoing bond, in case I find it satisfactory, and being so, in my opinion, by the present and on behalf of the Supreme Government of the Mexican Republic, I admit the said bond and declare that the Company has fully complied with the obligations imposed on it by Article 16th of the grant approved by the Congress of the Union the 29th December, 1868, and sanctioned by the Executive the 2d January, 1869.

(Signed) JOHN N. NAVARRO.

[SEAL.]

PART II

HISTORICAL AND GEOGRAPHICAL NOTES

1453—1869

By HENRY STEVENS, G M B, F S A, etc.
Fellow of the Royal Geog. Soc. of London, Cor Memb. Amer. Antiq. Soc. and of the Hist. Socs. of Mass. Conn. Maine, Vt. N. J. Penn. and Wiscon. and Blk Bld Athm Clb Lond.

D. Appleton & Co., New York, 1869.

Congress of Badajos.

I

HISTORICAL.*

A retrospect of four centuries, with a rapid glance at the progress of modern discovery, exploration, and invention, will probably serve as an appropriate introduction to our projected scheme of Interoceanic Communication by means of the TEHUANTEPEC RAILWAY, and show that the time is near at hand for its accomplishment. Let us, therefore, go back for a moment, and survey the little old world and its inhabitants as they appeared about the middle of the fifteenth century. According to Ptolemy, the best recognized authority, whose geography had stood the test of thirteen hundred years, the then known world was a strip of some seventy degrees wide, mostly north of the equator, with Cadiz on the west, and farthest India or Cathay on the east, lying between the frozen and the burning zones, both impassable by man. The inhabitants, as far as known in Europe, were Christians and Mohamedans, the one sect about half the age of the other. Christendom, the elder, that once held considerable portions of Asia and Africa, had been driven back inch by

* This chapter was contributed by HENRY STEVENS, G M B; F S A, 4 Trafalgar Square, London, May 10, 1869.

inch, in spite of the Crusades, even from the Holy Land, the place of its birth, up into the northwest corner of Europe; and both in lands and people was outnumbered six to one by the followers of Mahomet. For seven hundred years the fairest provinces of Spain acknowledged the sway of the Moors, and the Mediterranean, from Jaffa to the Gates of Hercules, was under their control. The crescent was constantly encroaching on the cross; while Christendom, schismatic, dismayed, demoralized, and disheartened, seemed almost incapable of further resistance.

India beyond the Ganges, from the days of Moses, Alexander, and Aristotle, to say nothing of the geographers Pomponius Mela, Strabo, and Ptolemy, was deemed the land of promise, the abode of luxury, the source of wealth, and the home of the spices; but the routes of commerce thither, via Venice and Genoa, by the Red Sea, Egypt, the Nile, Arabia, Asia Minor, the Black and Caspian Seas, through Persia and Tartary, were one by one being closed to Christians. The profits of the overland carrying trade were mostly in the hands of the Arabians, who inherited it from the Romans; but Memphis, Thebes, and Cairo, that flourished by it, had declined as it fell off, and yielded to Alexandria nearer the sea. Finally, in 1453, Constantinople, the Christian city of Constantine, fell into the hands of the Turks, and with it the commerce of the Black Sea and the Bosphorus, the last of the old trading routes from the East to the West. Christendom for a time was disconsolate, and could only "pray for the contertition of the Turks." The whole of the carrying trade passed into the hands of middle men or agents, who passed goods without news, and India became more a land of mystery than ever; but this apparent misfortune proved to be the beginning of a new and brighter era.

The learned Christians of Constantinople, with nothing but their heads and their books, fled in exile into Italy, and became its schoolmasters. At once began there the revival of learning, which soon extended throughout the West. "Westward the star of empire takes its way." The Medici family of Italy, at Venice and Florence, welcomed these learned Greeks, and bought their precious manuscripts of ancient lore. The gunpowder of Europe had already silenced the Greek fire of Asia. On the Rhine the young printing press was just giving forth the first sheets. The compass and the astrolabe, recent inventions, began now to give confidence to mariners and teach them that, though the old paths of trade overland were closed, they might venture on new ones over sea. In 1453, in Western Europe there was no tea, no coffee, no tobacco, no Indian corn, no potatoes; and many of the necessities of our day were not even known as luxuries. Though the Crusades had failed in their immediate objects, they had exposed the secrets of the India trade, and the vast revenues of the Eastern cities. The manuscript travels of Marco Polo and Mandeville had found their way into the hands of thinking men. Venice was already waning, preparatory to yielding its trade to Portugal, the then most rising and active maritime power. Prince Henry the Navigator had still ten years to live to carry out his great schemes of discovery and exploration of the western coast of Africa. He was an ambitious student of geography, history, mathematics, astronomy, and navigation, and for almost forty years had stood alone. At the early age of fifteen he had a successful brush with the Moors at Ceuta, opposite Gibraltar ; and by 1418 had crept down the coast of Africa to Cape Nun, lat. 28° 40′, the southern boundary of Morocco. In 1434 his captains doubled Cape Boyador, and seven years after obtained from Pope Martin V a grant to the crown of Portugal of all he should discover from this cape to the Indies. In 1442 Rio del Oro was reached, and gold and negro slaves brought back. These were two real stimulants to Portuguese discovery, avarice, pride, and wealth, though the conversion of the infidels to Christianity, was, no doubt, a strong additional motive power. The reintroduction of negro slavery, and the part it soon played in commerce and the world's progress, may be ascribed to Prince Henry. He encouraged the traffic, which, with the love of gold and the hatred of the Moors, aroused his countrymen to his projects, and insured the promotion of discovery, in so much that by the time of the fall of Constantinople, his captains had reached Cape Verde, lat. 14° 45′ N, probably a few degrees beyond, and had exploded the old theory of a boiling belt about the equator.

In all ages there had been a prevailing notion that one might sail round Africa ; but when once it was demonstrated that Portuguese sailors could cross the equator and survive, Prince Henry's vague idea of reaching the land of spices by this route was confirmed. At all events, he was schooling hardy sailors, and training them for bolder work, so that soon after the date of the fall of Constantinople, Italy and Portugal had reached that turn for adventure and enterprise, which spread like wildfire throughout the other States of Europe, and caused the entire revolution in the commerce of the world.

In 1453, Columbus was a lad of six years at Genoa, Vespucci of two years at Florence, and John Cabot a youth at Venice. The new learning at once took deep root. When these three Italian boys became men, behold how changed! The sciences of mathematics, astronomy, and navigation had grown with their growth, and developed with marvelous rapidity. The press had spread broadcast the learning of the ancients. The secrets of the earth were inquired into and revealed. Many islands of the Atlantic had been discovered and described, and sailors knew the coasts of Europe and Africa from Iceland to Cape Verde. But, above all, the knowledge of the sphericity of our earth was no longer confined to philosophers. Alexander had told Aristotle what he knew of the East, and Aristotle had written down that there was but a small space of sea between Spain and the eastern coast of India. Strabo had said that nothing stood in the way of a westerly passage from Spain to India but the great breadth of the Atlantic Ocean; but Seneca said this sea might be passed in a few days with favorable winds. Pomponius Mela and Macrobius put in like testimony, with certain difficulties about passing burning zones, and the earth being shaped like an egg floating in water. All these opinions were rehashed and digested by Ptolemy of Alexandria, in the second century, who first properly reduced the globe into 360 degrees of latitude and longtitude. In latitude he was as correct as he was incorrect in his longitude. Roger Bacon, an Englishman, again summarized these theories in his *Opus Majus*, in the thirteenth century; and in the fifteenth century Pierre d'Ailly, a Frenchman, reviewed the whole question, bringing together the opinions of the ancient writers named, as well as the fathers of the church, including modern philosophers, travelers, and theologians, especially Roger Bacon, Marco Polo, and Gerson, and gave to the world his well-known *Imago Mundi*. This celebrated work, finished in 1410, was afterwards the guide, companion and friend of Columbus. The learned author was Provost of the ancient Ecclesiastical College of St Dié in Lorraine, away up in the Vosges Mountains, in the remotest corner of France. This was on the very spot where, nearly a century later, in the Gymnasium within the same precincts, a confraternity of some half dozen earnest students, lovers of geography, of whom the poet Mathias Ringman was the soul, in a little work called *Cosmographiæ Introductio*, printed there in May, 1507, suggested that the New World should be named AMERICA, after a man, inasmuch as Europe and Asia had been named after women. Thus a little mountain town of France first gave aid and comfort to Columbus and afterwards a name to the New World.

As early as 1474, Paul Toscanelli a learned physician of Florence, sent to Columbus the Chart of Marco Polo, and was in correspondence with him on these very subjects, showing that even then the plans of Columbus were maturing. In 1478, the great geographical work of Ptolmey, with the 27 beautiful copper plate maps, was printed at Rome, and about the same time many other of the ancient historians, poets, philosophers, mathematicians, and astronomers saw the light. The *Imago Mundi* was printed at Louvain, in 1483, and there still exists at Seville, Columbus' own copy, with many of his manuscript notes, discovered and described about forty years ago by our countryman, Washington Irving.

Meanwhile, the work of discovery and exploration was earnestly pursued by the Portuguese. In 1454 Prince Henry secured the services of Cadamosto, an intelligent Venetian, well acquainted with the trade of the East, and sent him down the coast of Africa, where he reduced the explorations and trade to order, and pushed southward the discoveries to Sierra Leone in 1463, the year of Henry's death, and the capture of Gibralter by Spain from the Moors. Kings Alphonso and John continued these discoveries with so much energy that, after passing Congo, the bold captain, Bartholomew Diaz, reached the Cape of Good Hope, and looked beyond it, in 1487, thus completing an exploration of some six thousand miles of coast line in seventy years. Bartholomew Columbus was in this expediton.

Meanwhile King John had sent overland through Egypt, Pedro de Covilham, to India and Eastern Africa to gain information and report. In 1487 he reported that he had visited Ormuz, Goa, Calicut, &c., and had seen pepper and ginger, and heard of cloves and cinnamon. He visited the eastern coast of Africa, went down as far as Sofala, and returning northward, sent a message to King John that he had learned for certain that if Diaz should pursue his course round Africa he would reach India over the Eastern Ocean via Sofala. This theoretical discovery of Covilham exactly coincided with the practical one of Diaz.

All these events were but leading up to the grandest discovery the world ever knew, but it is difficult to trace the precise origin and the gradual development of the plans of Columbus. We know, however, that at the early age of fourteen he went to sea, educated with small knowledge of Latin and less Greek; and in 1474, at the age of twenty-seven, was in correspondence with Toscanelli, and became the father of Diego, the boy for whom, some ten years later, he begged a night's lodging at the Convent of La Rabida. By the year 1487, when the mystery of a path to India around Africa was solved, he had not only completely worked out his great idea of sailing West to find the East; but had offered his services in carrying it out, first to his native city, Genoa, without success, and had two years before brought it to Spain from Portugal where his proposals had been openly spurned and ridiculed, but treacherously though unsuccessfully tested. It is tolerably certain that much of his time had been spent in active and practical maritime service, for he had been down the coast of Africa as far as El Mina; had resided at Porto Santo, one of the out-lying Portuguese islands of the Atlantic, the daughter of whose first governor had become his wife; had visited England and Iceland, and was acquainted with the whole of the Mediterranean. His brother Bartholomew had been a chart-maker at Lisbon, and was his advocate at the court of Henry VII. We know from the writings of his son Ferdinand that he was both a practical and a learned mathematician as well as navigator. He had read probably all the compilations named above, and his own experience, together with what he had learned from the Portuguese, had enabled him, with his Marco Polo in his pocket, to sift all the vague and contradictory notions of the ancients as to the Antipodes and the shape of our earth, as well as to cypher out a theory of his own. For seven long years, after being worn out and disgusted elsewhere, he danced attendance on the Spanish court, with no fortune but his idea; sometimes threadbare and barefooted, ever pressing his suit, never flagging in his confidence, questioned and ridiculed by commissions of geographers and scientific men, without ever being able to penetrate the conservative ignorance of the learned and the courtly, or, as he complained, to convince any one man how it was possible to sail west and reach the East. But Time was working for him then, as it is now for Interoceanic Communication.

The fortieth year from the fall of Constantinople, the forty-fifth of the age of Columbus, witnessed the death of Lorenzo de Medici; but other suns were rising. Copernicus, in the far north, was in his twentieth year; Erasmus, his twenty-fifth; Cortes, his seventh; and Luther, his tenth. Martin Behaim, the old geographer of the Azores, aged sixty-two, was home on a visit to his native city of Nuremberg, from which the tide of commerce was ebbing. Here, in 1492, he made his famous globe of the whole world, as if to lay down upon it all the knowledge (and all the ignorance) of the geography of the earth, preparatory to the opening of new books. The same eventful year witnessed the expulsion of the Moors from Spain, the opening of the Mediterranean, and the discovery of America. Mohamedanism received its first check, and Christendom received a New World. These three Italian boys were men. When Columbus had balanced his egg for Spain, it was easy for Vespucci and the Cabots to do it for Portugal and England. Italy, whose noble sons did this in foreign service, never acquired a foot of the newly discovered lands for herself, yet how much of the honor was and still is hers.

In 1493, within three months from the return of Columbus, Alexander VI, a Spaniard, a Pope of not a year's standing, wishing to reward Ferdinand and Isabella for their struggles in expelling the Moors, divided our globe into two parts, by a line of demarcation passing from pole to pole, one hundred leagues west of the Azores and Cape Verde islands, giving to Spain all she should discover within 180° to the west of it, leaving to Portugal all her African discoveries and the Indies for 180° east of it. But poor Portugal, that had been struggling seventy years in the dark in her circuitous route to India round Africa, jealous of the new short cut of Columbus, which had been offered to her and refused, protested against the position of this meridian. It was finally settled in the treaty of Tordesillas, of June, 1494, with the Pope's approval, that the line should stand at three hundred and seventy leagues west of the Azores. Had the King of Portugal's geographers and pilots advised him to contend for a line further east instead of further west, he would have received within his half the Moluccas and the other Spiceries. As some compensation for this geographical blunder, however, he secured a foothold in Brazil. Both nations were now running a race of discovery of India by divers routes. By India is here meant all the East beyond the Ganges, including China, Cathay, Japan, and the Spice Islands. The acquisitions of the Spanish were named the West Indies, while those of the Portuguese were called the East Indies.

Never was great discovery more modestly announced. "*A Letter of Christopher Columbus, to whom our age is much indebted, respecting the Islands of India beyond the Ganges lately discovered,*" dated February, 1493. Columbus thought his success complete. He aimed at Zipangu, or Japan, and, to his dying day in 1506, believed that he had found it nearly where his calculations had placed it, but never was man more mistaken, and never did mistake produce greater results. Believing our earth to be a globe, Columbus reasoned correctly that by sailing west he would come to the east of Marco Polo, but from want of knowledge of longitude, he, like everybody else, from Ptolemy down, was vastly deceived as to the size of the globe. From Cadiz to the Ganges the distance had been computed from the days of Alexander, but was always much overrated. From the Ganges to the Corea and Cathay, and thence to Zipangu fifteen hundred miles more, the distance was also exaggerated by Marco Polo. So that, still going east, the distance from Zipangu to Cadiz was calculated to be about equal to the space from Palos to Saint Domingo. Upon this error in longitude hung no doubt the problem of circumnavigating the globe, for had Columbus suspected the real distance to Japan by the west, he would never probably have ventured to penetrate the "sea of darkness," or have found sailors bold enough to accompany him. The actual distance from San Francisco to Hong Kong is nearly one-third more than Columbus had reckoned it from Spain to Cuba.

The sensation produced throughout Europe by this discovery of a short and direct route to India was great, but for nearly twenty years nobody suspected the truth. The simple letter of Columbus in various editions, in prose and verse, was about all that was published for ten years, but the intelligence gave a new impulse to maritime discovery and commercial enterprise. Columbus, with full honors, returned in 1493, with a well equipped fleet to explore his Archipelago. He returned to Spain in June, 1496. Juan de la Cosa went with him in this second voyage. The Portuguese now redoubled their energies, and, in 1497, Vasco da Gama, just ten years after Diaz' discovery of the Cape, circumnavigated Africa and reached Calcutta. The same year the Cabots, under a license of Henry VII, given in 1496, in trying for a short cut to Cathay by the northwest, discovered Newfoundland and other islands, and took possession, supposing them to be off China, and erected conjointly the flags of England and Venice, on the 24th of June, 1497. The next year Sebastian Cabot explored the coast from Labrador to Virginia, that is, as he expressed it, to the latitude of Gibraltar and the longitude of Cuba. These discoveries were in 1498 reported to the kings of Spain by their vigilant ambassador in London, with the remark that he had seen Cabot's chart, and would send home a copy of it. What steps followed it is difficult now to trace, but the result appears to be that Henry VII, never following up the discoveries after 1498, Sebastian Cabot remained quietly at home till the death of Henry, when he took service under the king of Spain, permitting his English and Venetian rights of discovery and plantation to lapse. Thus ended the first English and Venetian attempts to reach Cathay by the northwest.

On the 30th of May, 1498, in his third voyage, Columbus first touched the continent of America in Venezuela, though some still contend that Vespucci had anticipated him by nearly one year. He called it Paria, and reasoned himself into the belief that it was Paradise, whence our first parents had been driven. In 1499, Vicente Yañez Pinzon and Alonzo de Ojeda, private traders, with the latter of whom was Vespucci on his second voyage, visited Brazil under Spanish flags; and in 1500 Brazil was discovered accidentally (?) by Cabral, in that great fleet which the success of Gama had called forth. He was blown out of his course on his way to India, and took possession for the Portuguese. Portugal thus gained undisputed possession of Eastern Brazil by rule of ignorance of longitude, claiming it as hers because it was east of the line of demarcation. All the science of Spain at that time could not disprove this, and therefore Pinzon abandoned it to the Portuguese. The same year, the Portuguese hearing of the voyage of the Cabots, and probably suspecting irreverence in the English for Papal bull lines of demarcation, sent Gaspar Cortereal to follow in their track. Labrador was discovered, and laborers (slaves) brought back to Lisbon the 8th of October, 1501. A second voyage was made the next year by the same captain, but not returning with his ship, a third expedition was sent in search of him, under command of his brother. Of this last expedition nothing was ever heard, and thus ended the Portuguese attempts to reach Cathay by the northwest.

In 1501 New Granada, Darien, and Panama were taken possession of for the Spanish by Bastides, and in 1501–2 Vespucci explored the coast of Brazil for the Portuguese, down as far as 50° S. lat., within two or three degrees of the strait, and in 1502 there was published an account of his expedition under the title of *Mundus Novus.* The years 1502 to 1504 were occupied by Columbus in his fourth and last voyage, in which he was accompanied by his brother Bartholemew, and his son Ferdinando, who afterwards wrote a life of his father. He explored the coast of Veragua, still looking for the Ganges and inquiring for the home of the Grand Kahn. An account of this voyage, coming down to July 7, 1503, was printed at Venice in 1505.

In 1502 Valentim Fernandez, a German, attached to the household of the ex-queen of Portugal, edited and printed at Lisbon a collection of voyages in the Portuguese language, comprising Marco Polo, Nicolo Conti, Santo Stephano, &c., with a view of stirring up the people to a more lively interest in the commerce and navigation of the Indies. The success of Columbus and the Cabots is referred to, and the speedy return of Cortereal from the north, from his second voyage, is expected. This magnificent folio volume, the first important book (not biblical) printed in Portugal, must have had a powerful effect in drawing popular attention to the land of spices. It was the first collection of voyages printed in the vernacular tongue, and could be read by all the unlearned who had a penny to venture. It was translated into Spanish, and printed at Seville in 1503. No rarer books are now known to geographers. In May, 1507, the four voyages of Vespucci were published for the first time together, in Latin, at St Dié, in France, as stated above, as an appendage to a little work on cosmography, a science which now began to assume new and startling importance.

On the third of November, the same year, there was published in Italian, at Vicenza, a most important collection of voyages, under the title, *Countries newly discovered, and the New World of Albericus Vespucci*, containing accounts of the voyages of Cadamosto to Cape Verde, in 1454–5; of de Cintra to Senegal, in 1462; of Vasco da Gama, in 1497–1500; of Cabral, in 1500–1; of Columbus (three voyages); of Alonzo Negro and the Pinzons; of Vespucci (four voyages; of Cortereal, &c. This work was the next year, 1508, printed in Latin and German.

All these new geographical works hitherto printed, it will be perceived, pointed to the same thing, enlightenment of the public as to India beyond the Ganges, and how to go and trade thither. In 1508, for the first time in print, all these discoveries were collected and laid down in a beautiful copper-plate map, by Johann Ruysch, a German, who had probably* visited the new found islands with the Cabots, and knew well what he was doing. It appears in the Ptolemy of 1508, published at Rome, accompanied by *A new description of the world, and the new Navigation of the Ocean from Lisbon to India, by Marcus Beneventanus.* A careful study of this map and its descriptive text, if we exclude all subsequent publications, and look at the world as seen by the geographers of that day, will greatly aid us in clearing up many apparent inconsistencies.

There were three distinct and independent fields of discovery. First, the Archipelago of Columbus in the center, filling a space of above a thousand miles from north to south, and open to India. This part of the map was no doubt laid down from Columbus' own letter, the only authority, in 1507, existing in print. He had, indeed, coasted along Paria from Trinidad westward, in June, 1498, as Pinzon, Ojeda, and others had done subsequently, supposing it to be another large island, or part of the mainland of Cathay, but nothing of this had then been printed. Second, the *Mundus Novus* of Vespucci,

* Beneventanus says "Joannes vero Ruisch Germanus Geographorum meo judicio peritissimus, ac in pingendo orbe diligentissimus cujus adminiculo in hac lucubratiuncula usi sumus, dixit, se navigasse ab Albionis australi parte; et tamdiu quo ad subparallelum ab subæquatore ad boream subgradum, 53, pervenit; et in eo parallelo navigasse ad ortus littora per angulum noctis atque plures insulas lustrasse, quarum inferius descriptionem assignabimus." *Anglicè:* But John Ruysch, of Germany, in my judgment a most exact geographer, and a most painstaking one in delineating the globe, to whose aid in this little work I am indebted, has told me that he sailed from the south of England, and penetrated as far as the 53d degree of north latitude [straits of Belle Isle (?)], and on that parallel he sailed toward the shores of the East [Asia (?)], bearing a little northward, and explored many islands, the description of which I have given below.

being the eastern coast of South America from Darien to Upper Patagonia, one vast Island with an unknown background. The authority for this was what has since been called Vespucci's "Third Letter," first printed at the end of 1502, or probably early in 1503. And third, the discoveries of the Cabots and the Cortereals in the north, represented by them as part of the mainland of Asia. This is only Marco Polo's chart of Cathay extended considerably to the northeast, and modified by the experience, probably, of Ruysch himself, and the information he gathered from the Bristol men, when he was with them in 1497–8.*

---

* The chart of Juan de la Cosa, representing the then known world, bearing the date of 1500, is not overlooked, but its significance, so far as the coast line of the United States is concerned, has been so manifestly distorted by almost every one who has described it, from its discovery by Humboldt in the library of Baron Walckenaer, nearly forty years ago, down to the present day, that the writer hesitates to venture his opinion. But by long study and comparison of this with other early maps, especially those of Ruysch and Peter Martyr of 1508 and 1511, he is convinced that the coast line, from the most westerly of the five English flag-staffs marking the extent of Cabot's discoveries southward and westward, to a point west of Cuba, precisely like the map of Ruysch seven or eight years later, is laid down as the eastern coast of Cathay, from the map of Marco Polo. If our Maine friends, therefore, will place behind their red line border, Marco Polo's name *Mangi*, they will see that this territory is farther "down East" than is generally supposed, being indeed Eastern Asia. The word Cuba, instead of *Juana* the name given by Columbus, and the fact that it is represented as an island, may be accounted for by a circumstance mentioned by Peter Martyr, that it was customary to add to recent maps the new discoveries as they were made.

La Cosa perished in Ojeda's mad expedition in Dec., 1509. He was a clever fellow, and a great favorite, and used to boast that he knew more of the geography of the new lands than did Columbus himself. Indeed, of all others, says Peter Martyr in 1514, his charts were the most esteemed. His knowledge and experience were great, for he had been, between the years 1493 and 1509, on no less than six exploring expeditions, either as pilot or commander, with Columbus, Ojeda, Vespucci, and Bastides, and had visited repeatedly the entire coast, from Paria to Uraba, and thence on his own account, north to the mid-

Columbus had placed his discoveries in the Indian Archipelago beyond the Ganges, and the world accepted the names he gave to the separate islands. No new general name was required. Cabot's discoveries being also East, were so re-

---

dle of Yucatan, as well as most of the islands in Columbus' vast Archipelago. When with Bastides, in 1501–2, he found that the Portuguese were meddling on the wrong side of the line of demarcation, endeavoring, probably, to find a shorter route to Calcutta via Darien, and therefore, on his return to Spain, La Cosa was sent to Lisbon to remonstrate against this encroachment. He was there imprisoned and was not released till August, 1504. Nothing daunted, the next year, 1505–6, he went on an exploring and trading expedition of his own to Uraba and Panama, and on another similar one in 1507–8. On the 11th of November, 1509, he embarked with Ojeda from Hispaniola, and perished soon after. From this it will be seen that he might be in Spain, chart-making, from June to October, 1500; from September, 1502, to 1504, autumn (except when in prison in Lisbon); and again parts of the years 1506–7, as well as parts of 1508–9. He had, therefore, ample time to touch up his great chart of the world, which he made and dated in 1500. The date is positive, and there is probably no reason to doubt it. But that he did retouch it subsequently is apparent from many circumstances. In the first place, there are manifestly two distinct letterings, in what may be called thin and thick letters, probably all by the same hand, but written at considerable intervals. All the thin letters *may* have been put on in 1500, but it is impossible to believe that all the thick letterings could have been received or known in time to be recorded in that year. There are many other points for discussion, but as the writer has never had under his eye the original chart, but judges only from M. Jomard's excellent colored facsimile on three double elephant folio sheets, he feels that he is treading on ticklish ground. The fac-similies (greatly reduced in size) given by Humboldt, Ghillany, Lelewel, and other writers, are in many respects defective, and tend to mislead the student, inasmuch as the coloring, and the lines of latitude and longitude are left out. Some names are misplaced and others are misspelled, while many important ones are omitted altogether. Only the western sheet or third, is given (except by Humboldt). But it should not be forgotten that the chart is intended to represent, on a plain, the entire globe as far as known in 1500. There is a broad green border above and beyond the Ganges, showing that the northeast of Asia is *terra incognita.* But La Cosa had the same authorities up to the Polisacus river and bay, in latitude 52° north that Behaim had for his globe made in 1492. Hence the two works agree remarkably well, but La Cosa, taking advantage of the seven years progress in geography has attempted to complete Asia by cognized as he placed them, and required no new general name, but his names of particular localities, such as Terra Nova and Baccalaos, were adopted. But as to the *New World* described by Vespucci, the case is different. This large coun-

---

laying down its northeastern coast on the other side of the globe, from somewhere about Zaiton in the Corea, to and some thirty degrees eastward, beyond the Polsiacus river and bay, through the kingdoms of Gog and Magog, and thence by a dream line connecting Asia with the discoveries of the Cabots and the Cortereals. The Polisanchiu river of Fra Mauro in 1457 is the Polisacus of Ruysch and the Ptolemies of 1511, 1513, 1535, and 1540. These and the Posacus of Schoner, the Puluisangu of Ortelius and Pulisangu in later maps maps are probably the Amoor river of our day. At all events, the river and bay are in eastern Asia, are about 50° to 52° north latitude, and therefore, America on La Cosa's chart cannot extend further west than the left flagstaff, the meridian of Porto Rico. The three rivers on the three reduced facsimiles are not in the original map of La Cosa, and, on one of them, the important words, *Mar descubierta por Yngleses,* are placed too low down and half an inch too far west, thus conveying the idea that the English had discovered Mangi.

In short, La Cosa's coast line, from Cuba to the first flagstaff, was intended for Asia, and to this day answers better for Asia than America. The student, therefore, who is not clear on these points is liable to get the Polisacus (sometimes spelled Plisacus) Bay, the Gulf of Maine, Rio Gomez, Cathay, Memphramagog, Gog and Magog, Quinsay, Cape Cod, Rhode Island, New York, Zaiton, Zipangu, Capes Race and Henlopen, Mangi, Carolina, Ciambu, Florida, Chicora, Cuba, etc., into a beautiful muddle. This is no exaggeration. This utter confusion has been made by compilers and amateur geographers from the times of Hylacomilus, Apianus, Schoner, Laurence Fries, Orintius Fine, and Muenster, to the present day, and no doubt will continue so until geographers look more carefully into the chronology and bibliography of their subjects. With these explanations this map is perfectly intelligible, and is reconcilable with other good maps made since the discovery of the Pacific in 1513, when America first began to stand alone in geography independent of Asia. The question next to be asked is, how far west and south did Sebastian Cabot go in 1497–8? According to Ruysch, as far probably as Cape Sable. The remark of Peter Martyr, in 1515 (after their eyes were opened to the size and shape of the globe by the discovery of the Pacific), about Cabot's reaching on the American coast the latitude of Gibralter, and finding himself then on a meridian of longitude far enough west to leave Cuba on his left, is simply absurd, dilemmatize it as you will. Such a voyage would have landed him near Cincinnati.

try was undoubtedly new, and as his was the first description of it printed, his friends of the Vosges Mountains, lovers of geography, sought very properly, in 1507, to compliment him by giving it, instead, the beautiful name AMERICA. This was done without the knowledge of Vespucci, and was never intended to interfere with the just rights and claims of Columbus. The truth is, there was then no other book in print describing Brazil but Vespucci's very simple and interesting letter, written (but in what language it is doubtful) probably immediately after his return in September, 1502. He gave the country he described no name, but the translator into Latin, Jean Basin de Sandacourt, Canon of St Dié, entitled his little tract *Mundus Novus.* But time wore on, and the mistakes of the geographers, as well as those of Columbus and Vespucci, are made apparent.*

In 1505–6 Nicaragua, Honduras, and Yucatan were seen by De Solis and Pinzon, and in 1508 Juana (henceforth called Cuba) was circumnavigated by Ocampo, thus dispelling the doubt about its being Zipangu, or part of the main land of Asia. It was found to be a long, narrow island, extending east and west, and not north and

* A little book, hitherto unknown, written by Walter Lud, and printed at Strasburg in 1507, entitled *Speculi Orbis Declaratio,* discovered by the writer in 1862, has been the means of clearing up many unjust aspersions of historians against Vespucci, and explaining the true state of affairs. The book is now in the British Museum. The writer, after unsuccessful endeavors for two years to place it in America, at the end of March, 1864, had the great satisfaction of calling the attention of his friend, R. H. Major, Esq., to it, and pointing out to him the passages referring to the Vespucci books. How well Mr. Major has used these materials his excellent paper on the Manuscript Map of Leonardo da Vinci, printed in the *Archæologia,* and his admirable *Life of Prince Henry the Navigator,* abundantly show. The next year the writer called Monsieur Harrisse's attention to it, and in his *Bib. Am. Vet.* it appears, under No. 49.

south, like Zipangu. A strange confusion now began to seize the German geographers of Strasburg and Vienna. They made Cuba an island, and called it Isabella, and then transferred all the names from Isabella to a mainland, named usually, Terra de Cuba, connecting it with Paria (sometimes with and sometimes without a narrow strait), standing bolt upright, and extending to 45° north latitude, with a point like Florida, and a gulf to the west of it. This was still supposed to be part of Asia, but in reality existed only in the imaginations of the geographers, like Antilla and San Brandan. It holds on their maps about twenty names, some of which are found on Ruysch's large island or main land west of Spagnola, and all of which are found on early maps, especially on a Portuguese portolano described by Lelewel under date of 1501-4. It is in the Ptolemy of 1513, extending up to 45°, while on the globe of Schoner, of 1520, it reaches 51°, and is separated from Zipangu by five or six degrees of Balboa's newly discovered Pacific Ocean. Off to the northeast, in its proper latitude and longitude, most of these maps have Terra de Corte Real as a large island, extending probably as far as the Cabots and the Cortereals discovered—that is, as far west as the meredian of Porto Rico. Some maps have it Terra de Cuba, others Paria; and one, in the *Margarita Philosophica* of 1515, from a misreading of Columbus' first letter, Zoana Mela. This fancy continent grew in size for nearly a quarter of a century, and was hard to get rid of, but the explorations of Ayllon, Gomez, Verrazano, Cartier, and others, finally drove it from our geographies.

In 1512 Florida, up to Chicora, was explored by Ponce de Leon, but it is now certain that it had been discovered two or three years before, probably by private adventurers, but perhaps by Ocampo in his return voyage in 1508. At all events, it appears correctly laid down in the excellent map of Peter Martyr printed at Seville April 11, 1511, under the designation, *Isla de Beimeni.* This map, exhibiting an unbroken coast line from Cape Santa Cruz, in Brazil, to Cape Catoche, in Yucatan, with hints of continental lines from Florida northward and westward, and one due north of Yucatan, if studied by the light of Peter Martyr's tenth book of his second decade, dated December, 1514, will foreshadow an approaching eclipse of Spanish enterprise.

There is little doubt that, at the time of the publication of this most important map, the author was still under the belief that all these new main lands somehow pertained to the continent of Asia. It is true, he informs us that some philosophers, and he leaves us to infer that he was one of them, had their suspicions that Columbus was mistaken in his opinion of its being Cathay, that the globe was larger than Columbus supposed, and that he had not really reached the antipodes, or the kingdom of the Grand Khan. But when Columbus, in his fourth voyage, brought home some poppinjays, and exhibited their brilliant plumage at court, the good old gossiping letter writer acknowledged that the great Discoverer was right, that such beautiful birds could come only from the East. Hence, probably, on this map the lines west of Beimeni and north of Yucatan are dream lines from Marco Polo. Indeed, Peter Martyr says, in his first decade, finished in 1510 and printed shortly after, that all these provinces of Paria, Cariena, Canehiet, Cuquibacoa, Uraba, Veragua, and others, are supposed to pertain to the continent of India. Florida and Beimini forgotten by Marco Polo, and left out of his report! Shade of Sebastian Cabot!

In 1511 Cuba was settled under favorable auspices, and with Diego Velasquez as governor over well to do colonists, it became the base of operations for extensive explorations. On the 8th of February, 1517, Francisco Hernandez de Cordova, accompanied by Bernal Diaz del Castillo, he of the *True History*, and Antonio Alaminos as pilot, who as a boy had sailed with Columbus, set out on an exploring expedition to the west, to look for trade, gold, and the long-sought passage to the land of promise. He went by Cape Catoche, the Bay of Campeche, as far as Champoton, and returned. The next year, 1518, on the 5th of April, Juan de Grijalva set out on the same route, with a better fleet and fuller instructions, accompanied by Bernal Diaz, Pedro de Alvarado, and the ever faithful Palinurus, Alaminos. They visited Cozumel, Cape Catoche, Campeche, Rio Tabasco, Potonchan, and named the country New Spain. They went as far as Panuco. Alvarado was sent back with the sick and heaps of gold, but Grajalva himself did not return to Cuba till the 15th of November. The journal of this important expedition, kept by the chaplain, Diep, was first published in Italian by Zorzi, at Venice in 1520, as an appendage to the *Itinerario* of Varthema.

Three days after Grijalva's return, Hernando Cortes, on the 18th of November, 1518, with the instructions in his pocket, which the governor sought in vain to recall after the return and favorable report of Alvarado, embarked on that most wonderful expedition of modern history, but he did not really leave Cuba for Cozumel till the 10th of February, 1519. He followed the courses of Cordova and Grijalva till he reached Vera

Cruz. From thence he ascended the Grand Plateau, and what followed is known to all the world. In his Second Relation, dated 30th October, 1520, Cortes sent to the Emperor a map of the entire Gulf of Mexico, well laid down, which was printed for the first time in 1524, at Augsburg, where Charles V had resided. On this map are the names of all the places at which he touched from Yucatan along the coast as far as Vera Cruz. These are, in order, Santo Anton, Roca Partida, Rio de Grijalva, Rio de la Palma, Rio de dos botas, Caribes, Santo Andres, Rio de Cocuqualquo, Roca partida, Rio de Vanderas, Rio de Alvarado, P. de Sant Juan, Seville, Almeria, and San Pedro. The Rio de Cocuqualquo was surveyed for many miles, probably with the hope of finding an opening to the South Sea.

In 1519, Francisco Garay, the Governor of Jamaica, dispatched Alonzo Alvarez de Pineda to explore the keys and coasts of Florida, but owing to the reefs and contrary winds, he directed his way round by the northwest coast by Mobile Bay, and the Mississippi river to Vera Cruz, thus completing a full and careful survey of the Gulf of Mexico. But still the disappointing report to the home government of Old Spain was —no thoroughfare. Here was the eclipse. Portugal had gained a strong foothold of eight hundred miles on the coast of Brazil in consequence of removing the Line westward. In this way Spain became hemmed in between two lines of demarcation, the one the breath of the Pope, the other the Cordilleras of the new hemisphere, the one about as impassible as the other, to the Spanish mind.

Thus all these three fields of discovery had by degrees crept into one vast continent, extending from the Arctic to the Antarctic Circles, and, instead of being India, the land of fabulous treasures, it was an impassible barrier to the approach thither by the western route. In 1513, when Vespucci had been in his grave a year, and Columbus seven, Nunez de Balboa first saw the Pacific Ocean from the mountain tops of Panama, and soon after navigators began to realize that the land of spices was beyond another ocean, even more vast than the Atlantic itself. The beautiful name AMERICA now began to swallow up the conjunctives, to spread itself eventually all over the new hemisphere, by the same law that made the Libya of the Romans succumb to its younger and more beautifully named daughter, AFRICA.

But Spain, with her new Emperor, her Fonsacas, her Corteses, her Pizarros, her Almagros, her Don Quixotes, her affluent miseries, her newly awakened thirst for gold, her Christian zeal, and her jealous rivalry for possession of the Spiceries, was not the power to bend or break. She redoubled her energies, made laws for the regulation of her half of the world, and pious and unscrupulous as they were, systematized her efforts. She would not permit the Portuguese to seek a passage to their eastern possessions through her half by the way of the Isthmuses of America, and by the same rule she felt a delicacy in using their route by the Cape of Good Hope. Her ambassadors and agents in foreign countries manifested no such scruples.

In 1512 or earlier, Sebastian Cabot was seduced from England, and induced to take service, with his experience, in Spain; and the same year Juan de Solis, exploring the coast of South America, discovered Rio de la Plata. In 1515 he was again sent thither with a view of finding a passage to the South Sea, and thence to the

Moluccas. This expedition returned soon after in consequence of the death of de Solis, but it led the way to a successful one in 1519, under Magellan, a disaffected Portuguese gentleman who had served his country for five years in the Indies under Albuquerque, and understood well the secrets of the Eastern trade. In 1517, conjointly with his geographical and astronomical friend, Ruy Faleiro, another unrequited Portuguese, he offered his services to the Spanish court. At the same time these two friends proposed not only to prove that the Moluccas were within the Spanish lines of demarcation, but to discover a passage thither different from that used by the Portuguese. Their schemes were listened to, adopted, and carried out. The Straits of Magellan were discovered, the broad Pacific was crossed, the Ladrones and the Philippines were inspected, the Moluccas were passed through, the Cape of Good Hope was doubled on the homeward voyage, and the globe was circumnavigated, all in less than three years, from 1519 to 1522. Magellan lost his life, and only one of his five ships returned to tell the marvellous story. The magnitude of the enterprise was equalled only by the magnitude of the results. The globe for the first time began to assume its true character and size in the minds of men, and the minds of men began soon to grasp and utilize the results of this circumnavigation for the enlargement of trade and commerce, and for the benefit of geography, astronomy, mathematics, and the other sciences. This wonderful story, is it not told in a thousand books? The Spanish eclipse was now passed, and America stood boldly out as an independent hemisphere.

Meanwhile, the Spanish were timidly tempting their new ocean. The Pacific shores of Darien, Panama, and Veragua were explored in

1515 to 1517, as they had been a few years before on the north side, with a view of finding a water communication from ocean to ocean. Estevan Gomez, another decoyed Portuguese pilot in the service of Spain, who went with Magellan in 1519 as far as the Straits and there discreditably deserted him, returning to Spain in 1520, reported that, though a strait had been found by the admiral, it was too remote and too dangerous for use. It was resolved, therefore, to seek for the supposed isthmian passage by a more thorough examination of the coasts of the Pacific. Accordingly, in 1522, four vessels having been built at Panama, d'Avila and the pilot Nino set out to explore the coast from the Bay of San Miguel to the Gulf of Fonseca, expecting to find at the latter place a passage by water through to the Gulf of Honduras.

The same year Cortes, after having subjected the mighty barbaric empire of Montezuma, extending from the Atlantic to the Pacific, with characteristic energy set himself to work exploring to find a natural water passage, or to make an artificial one. He ordered four ships to be built at Zacatula, two for direct trade to the Moluccas, and two to search for the strait. The voyage to the Moluccas was postponed, but the search for the strait was prosecuted so vigorously that, between the expeditions of d'Avila and his own, every inlet was explored between Colima, in latitude 18½° North, and the Bay of San Miguel, a distance of above 2,500 miles of coast line, but of course, without finding any passage. The following year, 1523, Cortes dispatched five small vessels to reconnoitre the coasts from Florida northward, to seek for the passage connecting the two oceans. His plan was to send another fleet up the western coast, that they might meet somewhere north of the German geographers' fancy continent, or sail round it. Of course they never met.

In 1524, Pizarro and Almagro, the future conquerors of Peru, began their approaches thither from Panama, carrying with them always the impossible instructions to seek out the hidden passage, while they were looking for trade and searching for gold.

The Portuguese in India and the Spiceries, as well as at home, now seeing the inevitable conflict approaching, were thoroughly aroused to the importance of maintaining their rights. They openly asserted them, and pronounced this trade with the Moluccas by the Spanish an encroachment on their prior discoveries and possession, as well as a violation of the Papal Compact of 1494, and prepared themselves energetically for defence and offence. On the other hand, the Spaniards as openly declared that Magellan's fleet carried the first Christians to the Moluccas, and by friendly intercourse with the kings of those islands, reduced them to Christian subjection and brought back letters and tribute to Cæsar. Hence these kings and their people came under the protection of Charles V. Besides this, Spain claimed that the Moluccas were within the Spanish half, and were therefore doubly theirs. Accordingly great preparations were made to dispatch a fleet of six new ships to the Moluccas, to establish and protect trade. The Council of the Indies advised the Emperor to maintain this fleet there, and to take the Spiceries into his own hands, and carry on commerce and navigation thither through his own exclusive channels, either by the strait recently discovered by Magellan, or by some hidden one which *must* soon be disclosed (if any reliance could be placed in the geographers) in a more direct line through some one of the Isthmuses; or, failing that, by opening communication from the coast of the Pacific.

Matters thus waxing hot, King John of Portugal begged Charles V to delay dispatching his new fleet until the disputed points could be discussed and settled. Charles, who boasted that he had rather be right than rich, consented, and the ships were staid. These two Christian princes, who owned all the newly discovered and to be discovered parts of the whole world between them by deed of gift of the Pope, agreed to meet in Congress at Badajos by their representatives, to discuss and settle all matters in dispute about the division of their patrimony, and to define and stake out their lands and waters, both parties agreeing to abide by the decision of the Congress.

Accordingly, in the early spring of 1524, up went to this little border town four-and-twenty wise men, or thereabouts, chosen by each prince. They comprised the first judges, lawyers, mathematicians, astronomers, cosmographers, navigators and pilots of the land, among whose names were many honored now as then—such as Fernando Columbus, Sebastian Cabot, Estevan Gomez, Diego Ribero, etc. They were empowered to send for persons and papers, and did in reality have before them pilots, Papal bulls, treaties, royal grants and patents, log books, maps, charts, globes, itineraries, astronomical tables, the fathers of the church, ancient geographies and modern geographers, navigators with their compasses, quadrants, astrolabes, mathematical instruments, etc. (See the frontispiece, engraved by Jacob Colon, 1660). For two months they fenced, cyphered, debated, argued, protested, discussed, grumbled, quarrelled and almost fought, yet they could agree upon nothing.

Whereas in the treaty of 1494 the Portuguese claimed the right of placing the line farther west than 370 leagues from the Cape Verde Islands, while the Spaniards contended rather to carry it farther east than placed in the original bull, both parties now (so much does self-interest sometimes modify arguments of right) contended for the very opposite to their former arguments. The line, however, had been fixed and approved by the Pope in 1494, and therefore could not be altered by them. But as there were 150 miles between the most easterly and most westerly of the Cape Verde Islands, they discussed angrily as to which island the line should pass through, each party knowing that every mile the line was moved here to the east or west, it would necessarily have to be moved just so much at the antipodes, the real field in dispute.

The debates and proceedings of this Congress, as reported by Peter Martyr, Oviedo, and Gomara, are very amusing, but no regular joint decision could be reached, the Portuguese declining to subscribe to the verdict of the Spaniards, inasmuch as it deprived them of the Moluccas. So each party published and proclaimed its own decision, after the Congress broke up in confusion on the last day of May, 1524. It was, however, tacitly understood that the Moluccas fell to Spain, while Brazil, to the extent of two hundred leagues from Cape St. Augustine, fell to the Portuguese. The calculation of longitude was the *pons asinorum* of the Congress, the very problem that had deceived Columbus and other experienced navigators a quarter of a century before. At this time, let it be remembered, no geographer had given any hint of the fan-like shape of

North America, but all maps represent it as a narrow strip of land, like that from Panama to Tehuantepec, with the South Sea itself narrow running up to the west of it.

However, much good resulted from this first geographical Congress. The extent and breadth of the Pacific was appreciated, and the influence of the Congress was soon after seen in the greatly improved maps, globes, and charts. Many doubtful points in geography and navigation were cleared up on both sides of the globe, and the latitude and longitude of many places were defined. Indeed, on the new maps after this, all the discoveries actually made, up to 1524, were tolerably well laid down, but there was a deal of imposition left in the imaginary lines of those parts of the North American coast which had not yet been explored, that is, between Florida and Nova Scotia. These false lines were still used by the pilots of both Spain and Portugal, probably with a view of blinding the eyes of each other, or leading astray the outside barbarians of England, France, and Holland, who, though children of the Father, and given to trade and adventure, had no share in the Papal gratuity. The fact that all the coasts of South America, Panama, Nicaragua, Honduras, Yucatan, the Gulf of Mexico and Florida, as well as of the Pacific shores from the Gulf of San Miguel to Colima, that had been surveyed by the Spaniards up to this time, were well laid down, both as to latitude and longitude, proves almost to a certainty that the indefinite coast line of the United States was still imaginary, if not Asiatic. Indeed, the old wood-cut maps of 1513 and 1522 of the German geographers, with their ideal continent, Terra de Cuba, did service, without alteration in the Ptolemies, for a quarter of a century later.

The return of Magellan's ship Victoria in 1522 aroused the spirit of public and private enterprise throughout Spain. Innumerable schemes for developing commerce with the Orient, and making further explorations, were proposed and discussed. Every pilot, whether amateur or practical, had his card of the shortest route to the Indies. Of these schemes no less than six in 1523 and 1524 were adopted by the government, and promoted wholly or in part by public funds; viz., that of Cortes, of Loyasa, of Gomez, of Aillon, of Cabot, and of Saavedra. The impending conflict with Portugal called together the Congress of Badajos. That being over by the 1st of June, 1524, and resulting practically in favor of Spain, these several plans were matured as fast as practicable.

Cortes, the first and most active, had no sooner conquered Mexico and clenched his conquest than he began his exploration of the coasts of the Pacific. Without delay he sent Alvarado and other captains to the south and southeast, to bring into subjection the chiefs of the Province of Oaxaca and what is now called the Isthmus of Tehuantepec, and, shortly after, proceeded thither himself.

Ships were built on the Pacific side, but with many of the materials carted over from the Coatzacoalcos River. All the details of this scheme, from the 15th of May, 1522, to the 15th of October, 1524, are recorded in Cortes's Fourth Relation to the Emperor, printed at Toledo, October 20th, 1525. This Relation in Spain, with the reports of Alvarado and Godoy attached, gave still another impulse to the new speculations and enterprises, as it showed not only the practicability, but the probability of opening by artificial means a direct route to the Orient in a low latitude and good climate. Cortes was clear-headed and far-sighted enough to see that lines of commerce must be straight lines, and that the curves of the capes in high latitudes are only temporary matters of necessity. Indeed, so sanguine was Cortes on these points, that he planted his personal hopes and private fortune on and near this isthmus, as likely to become the Old World's highway for Oriental commerce. All the lands and private estates selected for himself and his posterity, and confirmed to him in 1529 by the Emperor, were located here in the Valley of Oaxaca, and near Tehuantepec. He was ennobled in 1529, taking his title, Marquis del Valle, from his possessions chosen here. To this day they are called the Cortes Estates, or the Marquisanas. He and his kinsman, Saavedra, had vast schemes for opening communication, by means of a ship canal or Roman road, for the transportation of merchandise brought hither from the Moluccas and other parts of the East for passage or transhipment to Spain. How unexpectedly this rational scheme was thwarted will appear farther on.

At the end of 1524 or early in 1525, Estevan Gomez, the pilot, who had been in the east, had started with Magellan and deserted him, a delegate to the Congress of Badajos, was the first to get off from Spain. He had boasted that he could find a passage to Cathay and the Spice Islands by the north, as Magellan had done by the south. He must have seen at Badajos, if not before, the maps of Ruysch, with the continent west of Spagnola extending to 35° north, and the Hilacomylus map of 1513, carrying the same ideal continent up to lat. 46°, ending with Cape Mar del Oceano, just above Ruysch's Cape Helicon (probably named from the rumored fountains of Florida). Peter Martyr's map of 1511, and Cortes' map of 1520, printed in March, 1524, together with the knowledge that Ponce de Leon, in 1512, and Aillon, in 1520, had explored the coast of Florida up to 33°, a little above Charleston; and it being known that Aillon had another commission in his pocket, dated June 12, 1523, to explore still further north of Florida; and his own commission being to find a strait between Florida and Bacalaos; these considerations make it probable that Gomez' field of search lay between 35° and 45°, or between Norfolk and Cape Sable, where, as Peter Martyr expresses it, "he found pleasant and profitable countries agreeable with our parallels." Very little is known about this unimportant expedition, and no authentic maps or papers have come down to us. The contemporary historians give no prominence to it, and very few facts about it. Indeed, from what is at present known, it is very difficult to tell whether he sailed up or down the coast, or both, or at what points he touched. So little information did he bring back, that it would not now be a matter worth discussing, if the results of the voyage had not been so enormously exaggerated by recent writers.

Let it be borne in mind that Gomez sailed with only a single caravel of fifty tons, with perhaps a dozen men, in the dead of winter, from Coruna, in lat. 43°, the government contribution towards the cost of the fit-out being only 750 ducats, returning in November, 1525, after an absence of about ten months, with some Indian slaves, whom he had kidnapped against a recent law of Spain and the positive instructions of the Emperor, and you have the whole story. Oviedo, writing in 1526, says that he sailed to the northern parts and found a great part of land continuate from that which is called Bacalaos, taking his course towards the west to 40° and 41°, from whence he brought certain Indians. Would an intelligent pilot sail north with such a craft in winter? Might not New England be the "great part" of land next to Bacalaos; and might not the fine tall natives of Rhode Island have been kidnapped, part being taken to Cuba for sale, the rest taken to Toledo, thus consuming the ten months, without having gone north of Cape Cod? Peter Martyr says, writing also in 1526: "He, neither finding the strait nor Cathay, which he promised, returned back within ten months from his departure. I always thought and presupposed this good man's imaginations were vain and frivolous." Herrera, who wrote three quarters of a century later, is hardly more favorable to this explorer.

The reader is referred, by recent writers, to the manuscript map of Ribero of 1529, now preserved at Weimar, for the result of Gomez' voyage. But the intelligent reader will see with half an eye that this is a partizan map, and intentionally deceptive in the coast line between 33° 40′ and 50° N. The discoveries of the English are thrown into Greenland, and called Labrador, while Bacalaos is given to the Portuguese, and cut off by the line of demarcation. All the rest of the coast is closed up under the names of Gomez and Aillon, and so given to Spain. There is no room left for the discoveries of Verazzano for the French in 1524. The Spaniards knew of his voyages, for they had been watching him, had caught him, and in 1527 hanged him as a corsair. Indeed, the best that can be reasonably said of the voyage of Gomez is, that it exploded the ideal continent of the German geographers, and, connecting the explorations of Aillon with New

England, showed that the coast of North America trended continually eastward, so as probably to connect it with the discoveries of the Cabots, and thus make the whole coast west of the Line Spanish.

Lucas Vasquez Aillon, a lawyer, a Senator in Hispaniola, and a man of position, immediately after the survey of the entire Gulf of Mexico under Grijalva and Cortes, went up the coast of Florida in 1520, as far as Chicora, exploring beyond the limit of Ponce de Leon, as far, probably, as Cape Fear, seeking for the passage to Cathay. He found a fine country, but to Asia no throughfare. The next year he returned to Spain, and was, according to Peter Martyr, in behalf of the Regency of Hispaniola "a long time suitor [to the Council of the Indies] to have leave to depart again into those countries, to build a colony there." At length, after the return of Magellan's ship Victoria with its glorious news, the Council granted his request, and articles of agreement were signed the 12th of June, 1523, giving him permission, at his own expense, to fit out as many vessels as he pleased for the purpose of planting his proposed colony, but the usual instructions were inserted in his grant, to explore all inlets and islands with a view of finding a passage to Cathay. This license, given by Navarrete, permitted him to explore as far as 800 leagues to the north from Hispaniola. He returned to Hispaniola, built there six fine vessels, and, after many delays, sailed with them and above 500 men and nearly 100 horses, in July, 1526. He went as far north as lat. 33° 40′, found no strait, and met with nothing but misfortunes. The 18th of October Aillon died, and soon after the few survivors, about 150 out of the 500, returned to Hispaniola, the expedition being a dead failure. Thus ended the attempt to plant a colony near the mouth of Cape Fear River, and thus ended the Spanish attempt to penetrate to the East by the way of the North. Both Gomez and Aillon had found no gold, and no strait, and even the trees and the animals they reported were common in Europe; whereat old Martyr exclaims, "to the south! to the south! for the great and exceeding riches of the equinoctial; they that seek riches must not go unto the cold and frozen north." The whole story is comprehended in Martyr's sentence. North America, by the Spaniards, was never considered of any consequence of itself, and was regarded only as a barrier or a stepping stone to a richer, older and better land. It was necessary, however, to shut it up by a coast line west of the line of demarcation, so that other nations might be deterred from finding a northern passage to India.

The Emperor, considering the verdict of the Congress of Badajos in his favor, lost no time in dispatching his new fleet of six sail and 450 men by the Straits of Magellan, from Coruna, on the 24th of July, 1525, under the command of Loyasa, to the Moluccas and the Spice Islands, with the view, first, to succor the men left there by Magellan's fleet, and then to establish a government bureau and to protect its commerce. The Straits were passed, and four of the six ships reached the Moluccas; but the story of their long, long sufferings is too long to be told here.

In April, 1526, Sebastian Cabot, who had for years been the Pilot Major of Spain—said, however, to have been a better cosmographer than pilot—after long and ample preparations at Seville, sailed for the Moluccas via the Straits of Magellan, with four well-equipped ships, for the purpose of reinforcing and assisting the expedition of Loyasa. This expedition was another dead failure. For some unaccountable reason,

Cabot did not deem it prudent to try the Straits of Magellan, but attempted to find a passage through the Rio de la Plata. He penetrated far into the interior of Paraguay, explored many large rivers and fertile provinces, suffered many hardships, lost most of his men and ships, and finally, after four years of toil and disappointment, returned without any favorable results.

Cortes was kept informed of these several expeditions, with a request from the Emperor that he would cooperate with them at the Moluccas, by sending a fleet from the western coast of Mexico. Accordingly he caused three ships to be built on the Pacific, and dispatched them, with 110 men and thirty pieces of artillery, under command of his kinsman, Saavedra, from some port of Southern Mexico, probably Tehuantepec, Huatulco, or Acapulco, on the 31st of October, 1527. This fleet met that of Loyasa in the Moluccas, cooperated with it, found the Portuguese strong and resolute, by no means disposed to abandon the islands, fought them separately, and fought them together for months, nay, for years, never hearing a word from home, being cruelly neglected, yet loyal and true, till, reduced to a handful, some few of the survivors, long after Loyasa and Saavedra had died, as well as most of the sub-officers, found their way home after twelve years of unspeakable hardships. Thus all these six hopeful expeditions brought nothing but disappointment. The Straits of Magellan were found so dangerous and remote, that old Peter, had he lived, would no doubt have again exclaimed as before, "To the north! to the north! they that seek riches must not go to the dangerous and frozen south!"

As early as 1526 or 1527, before the extent of these failures was known, it became apparent, if the commerce of the East was to flourish, it must be by some more direct communication. These great difficulties of the extreme North and South determined the Spaniards to explore the Isthmuses yet more thoroughly. All the five routes, from Darien to Tehuantepec, were spoken of then as now, with the view of constructing immediately a canal, road, or portage, deeming it safer and cheaper to tranship goods, than to carry them round by the Strait. "These are mountains it is true," exclaimed the old historian, "but Spanish hands, and Spanish enterprise can overcome them." But no Spanish hands could overcome the impolitic blunders of the Emperor. There is little doubt that interoceanic communication would have been opened in 1529 or 1530, by means of a ship canal or a turnpike across the Isthmus of Tehuantepec, had not the Emperor, who was greatly in want of money, defeated all the schemes, against the advice of the Council of the Indies, by pawning to the King of Portugal, who had just married his sister, the Moluccas for 350,000 ducats. So the trade of the Moluccas passing for a time out of the hands of the Spaniards, there was no immediate pressure for the completion of this great work. The opportunity then lost of securing an exclusive transit was never recovered by Spain, but it is reserved to us of to-day to make the ISTHMUS OF TEHUANTEPEC the world's highway.

H. S.

May 10, 1869.

ERRATA. Let him that is not without *errata* in his own life correct neatly with his pen, and pardon these of mine: Page 13, line 23, for Cuba, *read* Japan; Page 14, line 9, for Virginia, *read* the south; Page 24, line 27, for Diep, *read* Dies; Page 29, line 29, for theirs, *read* hers; Page 32, line 7, for was, *read* were; and also, any others that his quick eye may detect. The writer will reciprocate with opportunity.

II.

TOPOGRAPHY OF THE ISTHMUS.

The Isthmus of Tehuantepec is that portion of the Mexican territory which lies between the Gulf of Mexico and the Pacific Ocean, where the two seas approach the nearest to each other, and comprises the eastern portion of the States of Vera Cruz and Oaxaca, or the extreme southern portion of Mexico, bordering upon Central America.

From the mouth of the Goatzacoalcos, which discharges itself into the Gulf in 18° 8′ 20″ north latitude, and 94° 32′ 50″ longitude west (from Greenwich), to the harbor of Ventosa, on the Pacific, situated in 16° 11′ 45″ north latitude, and 95° 15′ 40″ west longitude, the distance in a direct line is 143½ miles. The coast-lines on either side have a general direction nearly east and west.

In considering the Isthmus with reference to its general topographical features, it may properly be said to comprise three main divisions, more or less distinct in their general characteristics: the first, embracing that portion extending from the Gulf to the base of the Cordillera, and which may be called the *Atlantic plains;* the second, comprising the more elevated or *mountainous districts* in the central parts; and the third, including the level country bordering the ocean on the south, and known as the *Pacific plains.*

The first division comprises a belt of country of some forty or fifty miles in breadth, lying contiguous to the Gulf coast, and made up of extensive alluvial basins of exceeding richness and fertility, through which the drainage of the northern slope of the Cordillera discharges itself into the Gulf.

The principal of these hydrographic basins is that of the Goatzacoalcos, which occupies the central portion of this division, and has a general direction of N.N.E. by S.S.W. It is separated from the basin of the Tonala and Tancochapa rivers on the east, and the San Juan on the west, by a moderately elevated plateau or table land, furrowed by numerous small streams, and generally covered with dense forests. These table lands, with few exceptions, are not elevated more than two or three hundred feet above the sea level.

With the few exceptions here referred to, the entire country embraced in the northern division presents the appearance of a broad plain entirely covered with dense forests.

The second or middle division may be said to extend from the Jaltepec River on the north to within twenty or twenty-five miles of the Pacific coast, comprising a strip of country through the central portions of the Isthmus, of some forty miles in breadth on the west, and gradually widening out towards the east to sixty or seventy miles. This division presents a great diversity of feature. The immense chain of the Cordillera, which under different denominations extends almost without interruption the entire length of the two Americas, traverses the country from east to west; but instead of those lofty volcanic peaks, which constitute so striking a feature of extensive portions of this gigantic chain of mountains, there is a sudden depression of the range in its passage across this isthmus, the continuity of the chain being nearly broken at a point directly in the line of shortest communication between the two oceans. The Cordillera here approaches very near the Pacific coast, and its southern slope terminating suddenly, extends in nearly a right line for a considerable distance in an east and west direction.

The elevated spurs and ridges, which traverse the

country generally in an east and west direction, offer the principal obstacles to the construction of a railroad across this portion of the Isthmus. The mountain range gradually becomes more elevated as we approach the Summit Pass, and presents a more uniform level surface, bounded on the south by the cerros Prieto, Masahuita, and Espinosa, which terminate in rugged limestone peaks, at an elevation of from 1,500 to 2,000 feet above the Pacific.

By a narrow opening or gap in these mountains we descend suddenly from the elevated table lands to the Pacific plains, which form the third or southern division. These plains average about twenty miles in breadth, from the base of the mountains to the Pacific coast, and descend to the lagoons at an inclination varying from ten to fifteen feet in the mile, thus forming as it were an immense inclined plane, with its side next the mountains about two hundred and fifty feet above the Pacific. Under these circumstances they present a remarkably smooth, even surface, with a uniform, gentle slope towards the sea. In some instances there are occasional isolated hills, which, rising abruptly, form a prominent feature in the topography of this part of the country. The plains are traversed by eight rivers, which discharge the drainage of the southern slope into the sea. Seven of these rivers empty into the lagoons, which are connected with the sea by a narrow outlet called the Boca Barra; the eighth, or Tehuantepec River, comes from a northwesterly direction, and passing through the city of the same name, discharges itself directly into the sea at the Bay of Ventosa.

The most important of the streams referred to, as respects length and the volume of their waters, are the Ostuta and Chicapa on the east, and the Tehuantepec on the west. The first two named rivers have their source in the highest parts of the Sierra, to the east of San Miguel Chimalapa. These streams derive their chief importance as being the source from which a sufficient supply of water may probably be obtained for the summit level of a ship canal.*

All of these streams as they issue from the mountains are remarkably pure and limpid, even in times of flood, thereby indicating the rocky nature of the districts which they drain. In their descent towards the plains they offer almost unlimited sources of water power, which at many points may be made available for sawing lumber or for other purposes.

The Bay of Ventosa is formed by an indentation in the coast, and the projection of the Cerro Moro on the west. The Tehuantepec River discharges itself near this point. The bay is partially sheltered from the north winds by low ranges of hills from three to four miles distant. A short distance to the westward are two similar indentations of the coast, known respectively as Salina Cruz and Salina del Marques.†

Of the streams watering the northern slope of the Isthmus, the most important by far is the Goatzacoalcos,‡ by reason both of the comparatively large extent of country for the drainage of which it is the outlet, and also as furnishing the natural channel through

---

* The surveys for this canal were executed in 1842, under Señor G. Moro, with every means at his command for arriving at a correct result, and he determined the entire practicability of the scheme, which will be noticed in the proper place.

† For a detailed description of Ventosa, vide page

‡ Many disputes have arisen with regard to the orthography of this name. In the official dispatches of Hernan Cortes to the Emperor Charles V., he writes it in no less than six different ways, viz.: "*Mazamalco,*" "*Quacalco,*" "*Cuacuacalco,*" "*Cuicicacalco,*" "*Guazacualco,*" and "*Guazaqualco.*" The veteran soldier Bernal Diaz del Castillo, who resided more than thirty years in the province, calls it "*Cuasualco.*" De Solis, on the other hand, writes it "*Goatzacoalcos*;" and the Abbé Clavigero, who, from his extensive knowledge of the languages of Mexico, is perhaps the best authority, writes it after this manner, viz.: "*Coatzacualco.*" We have followed De Solis, as in accordance with the letter of the grant and the prevailing custom of official papers at this date.

which the projected communication between the two oceans may in part be effected. This river takes its rise in the unexplored part of the Sierra to the east of Santa Maria Chimalapa. Its principal tributaries are the Chichihua and Almaloya. The latter takes its course through the plains of Chívela, and derives its chief importance as probably furnishing the most feasible route by which the railroad may be carried to these plains from the north.

The rivers Sarabia, Jumuapa, and Jaltepec (or de los Mijes) enter the Goatzacoalcos on the left bank, and next to them the Chalchijapa on the right. The first two descend from the Sierra of Santa Maria Guinenagate; and although the Sarabia carries a considerable volume of water, it is not navigable. The Jaltepec River has its source in the Sierra of the Mijes. This river is nearly as large as the Goatzacoalcos above the confluence of the two streams, and is the most important tributary on the west.

Above the confluence of the Jaltepec, the country on either side of the Goatzacoalcos is more or less broken and hilly, and the banks of the stream often rocky and precipitous; but below this point the margins are comparatively low, and the surface level for some distance back from the river.

Below the island of Tacamichapa, the Goatzacoalcos receives the waters of the Coachapa River on the east. The source of this stream is unknown, but it has been ascended in canoes for twelve days, the time usually occupied in going from the bar of the Goatzacoalcos to the Pass of Sarabia; schooners have also sailed up it for some distance. The cross-ties used on the railroad at Vera Cruz were manufactured from timber obtained from the banks of this stream.

Four miles below the debouche of the Coachapa, but on the opposite shore, is the village of Minatitlan, and three miles below this the river Uspanapa joins the Goatzacoalcos by its right bank.

The Uspanapa is the most considerable of all the

numerous tributaries of the Goatzacoalcos, and is in some respects even superior to the latter stream for purposes of navigation, carrying a sufficient depth of water to float large vessels to a greater distance from the Gulf, and being also less tortuous. The Indians assert that it has been ascended in canoes for twenty-five days, but it was probably never explored by them to its source. The mountains near the head waters of this stream have the reputation of being rich in gold and silver mines.

The banks of the river below Minatitlan are very low, and frequently flooded. The mouth of the Goatzacoalcos, the geographical position of which has been given, is one hundred and fifteen miles west from the river Grijalva or Tabasco, and about one hundred and ten miles from Vera Cruz. Its width is about fifteen hundred feet, and its depth varies in different places.

III.

INHABITANTS.

The Isthmus of Tehuantepec comprises within its limits a mixed and heterogeneous population, consisting of *Europeans*, *Creoles*, *Mestizos*, *Indians*, *Mulattoes*, *Zambos*, and *Negroes*.

The *European* portion, numerically considered, is exceedingly insignificant; embracing only a small remnant of French colonists, with a few German adventurers, and some old Spanish settlers, dispersed over various localities. They control almost the entire trade of the Isthmus, and, with few exceptions, are the only mechanics and tradesmen to be found.

The *Creoles* (the descendants of the Conquistadores and other Europeans) compose the native white population, and are somewhat more numerous. On the southern portion of the Isthmus, where they principally reside, they are found holding all the civil and military appointments. Although the landed wealth of the country is mostly in their hands, they are far from being individually rich; and there is, perhaps, no social organization in which the extremes of wealth and the extremes of poverty so often meet. The difference in color is made the criterion of respectability. With few exceptions, they exclusively possess the little amount of learning which is disseminated over the Isthmus—a circumstance that helps to define, with rigid accuracy, the boundaries of social distinction.

The *Mestizos*, in point of influence, may be justly considered next; the more especially "where rank depends more on the complexion than on endowments, and where almost every shade has its limits defined by terms which, though apparently only expressing the color, in reality express the rank of the individual." This division of the inhabitants has become an important part of its population, and constitute what may be appropriately denominated the middle class. As such, many of them are prominent men, and enjoy the advantages of comparative wealth and education. The Mestizos are scattered over almost all parts of the Isthmus, and comprise the *mayordomos*, the *mayorales* of the haciendas, the *arrieros* of the mule trains, and the under officials of the custom-house, and of the municipal police. They are characterized by habits of industry, but not of strict sobriety.

The *Indians*, who are by far the most numerous portion of the inhabitants, comprehend the remnants of various once powerful tribes, which, notwithstanding the changes and vicissitudes that have marked their condition since the days of the Conquest, still exhibit distinctive characteristics sufficient to identify the sources from which they originally sprung. Among these are the *Aztecs*, *Agualulcos*, *Mijes*, *Zoques*, *Zapotecos*, and *Huaves*. These are distributed over the country in a manner which corresponds somewhat with its peculiar topographical divisions.

On the northern part of the Isthmus, within the intendency of Vera Cruz, and extending as far south as Mt. Encantada (beyond which, to the Rio Sarabia, a broad belt of uninhabited country intervenes), are found the Aztecs and Agualulcos. Whatever peculiarities may have existed in the idiomatic structure of the native languages of the Isthmus, it is certain that they are now little else than mere ill-spoken dialects, replete with corrupt and broken sentences of Spanish.

In their persons the Indians are somewhat below the medium stature, but squarely built, and of great muscular strength, being often able to support a weight of from one hundred and fifty to two hundred and fifty pounds on their shoulders for several hours, exposed to the rays of the hottest summer sun. They are copper-colored, with smooth, coarse hair, small beard, diminutive eyes, prominent cheek-bones, low, narrow forehead, aquiline features, white teeth, thick lips, and a gentle expression of mouth, strongly contracted, with a melancholic and severe look. The women, on the other hand, are less strongly built, and in some instances beautiful and well proportioned—a beauty which is enhanced by the natural grace of their carriage. Their movements are quick and mercurial, and their manners are characterized by shyness rather than modesty.

The Abbé Clavigero, in his excellent work on Mexico, says, in reference to the physical character of the Indians, that "there is scarcely a nation perhaps on earth in which there are fewer persons deformed; and it would be more difficult to find a single humpbacked, lame, or squint-eyed man amongst a thousand Mexicans, than among any hundred of any other nation." This assertion is literally true of the natives on the Isthmus. In their habits they are exceedingly simple, and their chief subsistence consists of vegetable food. As a general rule, they are little inclined to work; but, from the natural docility of their character, it seems only reasonable to infer that under better and brighter circumstances they would become both useful and industrious. Every man and boy wears a *machete*, and the facility and dexterity of its use is not a little surprising. It serves as a weapon for defence, an instrument for killing beef, an axe for cutting wood, and a knife for eating, &c. As axemen, to perform the grubbing and clearing on the route of the proposed railroad, their services will be found invaluable.

Their amusements are scarcely worthy of note. In fact, an atmosphere of apathy seems to pervade every thing, and even their liveliest songs are sad, and their merriest music melancholy.

In religious matters they are reverential but superstitious; and the ceremonies of the church, with its numerous *fiestas* and processions, are loved because they are gloomy and peculiar.

As a cultivator, the Indian is poor, but he is free; and he loves the solitude of his wretched *ranchito*, because it restores him, even as a peon, some of the long-lost liberty of his ancient race. This desire for solitude has given rise to that disposition among them to inhabit the elevated sections and summits, and to locate their *pueblos* on sites less convenient of access, and less advantageous to prosperity.

Everywhere on the Isthmus—even on the loftiest mountains, in the deepest dells, and in the most impenetrable forests—there are silent evidences of the history of a vast and powerful people, of which there scarcely remains now a tenth part, as the miserable consequence of their calamities.

The Indians on the northern part of the Isthmus evince the greatest veneration for the memory of Doña Marina, the beautiful mistress of Cortes. In her native village of Painalla, now called Jaltipan, a large circular mound of earth, known as the "Hill of Malinche," serves to recall the history of her imperishable deeds. Among the Indians, there is still preserved a tradition that her remains are buried beneath it, and that she promised to return from the captivity of death, to sweep from their thresholds the blight which she had involuntarily aided to bring. Who, then, can say that the traditionary dream of the Indian, as he veils the pangs of his heart under the deceitful guises of indifference and stupidity, is not already on the eve of realization, and that the ancient province of Goatzacoalcos, which through an humble captive slave exerted so powerful an influence over the commercial destinies of the world, may not again break forth from its sleep to effect changes far more lasting and glorious?

The *Mijes*, once a powerful tribe, inhabit the mountains to the west, in the central division of the Isthmus, and are now confined to the town of San Juan Guichicovi.

The *Zoques* inhabit the mountainous region to the east, from the valley of the Chicapa on the south, to the Rio del Corte on the north. At present they are confined to the villages of San Miguel and Santa Maria Chimalapa. In some of their characteristics they are similar to the Mijes, but more athletic, and easily distinguished by the prominence of their features and the singular custom they have of shaving the crown of the head. Like the Guichicovi Indians, their knowledge of Spanish is limited.

The *Zapotecos* constitute the greater part of the population of the southern division of the Isthmus, and are incomparably superior to those of any other portion. The salubrity of the climate, the surpassing fertility of the soil, and the variety and richness of its productions, all minister to the prosperity of the inhabitants, who have from the most remote periods of their history been distinguished for their advances in civilization.

Intellectually, the aborigines of Tehuantepec exhibit qualities of no mean order, and they are found intelligent, docile, and lively. In personal appearance, they are noted for the symmetry of their forms, the singularity of their features, and the vigor and sprightliness of their character. The women are delicately made, mercurial, voluptuous, and full of vivacity. They are particularly remarkable for the exquisite grace of their carriage, the winning softness of their manner of expression, and their love of gay costumes. In morals, they are full of intrigue; but in habits, they are temperate and industrious.

The Indians of Juchitan, though numerically less than those of Tehuantepec, form an important part of the inhabitants of the Isthmus, as being superior in every respect. They are bold, independent, industrious, and temperate, possessing great muscular strength and a high degree of mental capacity. Of the value of their services, either as laborers in the construction of works, or as cultivators in the field, there can be no question.

The *Huaves*, who, according to their traditions, came originally from Peru, and once a powerful race, have, from their successive struggles for supremacy with the Zapotecos and Mijes, dwindled down to a little more than three thousand, scattered over the sandy peninsulas formed by the lakes and the Pacific. At present they occupy the four villages of San Mateo, Santa Maria, San Dionisio, and San Francisco.

The few *Mulattoes* who are scattered over the Isthmus, are the descendants of the native whites and the liberated slaves of the estates of the Marquesanas. They are generally robust and industrious, applying themselves to the cultivation of indigo and cochineal.

The *Zambos*, a half-caste between the Indian and the Negro, are found principally at El Barrio, Tarifa, and Niltepec. They inherit few good qualities, and are neither intelligent, industrious, or sober.

The *Negro* population is so insignificant that they

scarcely claim attention. In some few instances, however, they are hard-working and deserving people.

In a retrospective view of the character and condition of the inhabitants of the Isthmus of Tehuantepec, there is little to excite our admiration, but much to pity and deplore; yet amid the atmosphere of degradation, ignorance, and depravity which overshadows the land, there are refreshing hopes that promise, under careful culture, to yield an abundant harvest. They seem to need only the example of activity to rekindle their dormant energies, and the neigh of the "iron horse" to awaken them from their indolent dream.

IV.

CLIMATE.

As a regular mountain chain the Andes may be said to descend suddenly at Panama, and are merely continued northward to join the Rocky Mountains by a mass of elevated ground, with an irregular mixture of mountains and table land. This table land commences at the Isthmus of Tehuantepec, and passes northwest to latitude 42°, an extent of 1600 miles.

The result of this conformation is to give to the Isthmus the full benefit of the coast winds and rains from the north, which play over three-fourths of the breadth of land, and are only retarded from passing across its whole extent by the mountain land. There is thus a free circulation of air across the whole Isthmus, sweeping through the valley of Chicapa, and carrying the cool air of the north across to the Pacific shore.

"On the Isthmus there are but two seasons, winter and summer. In winter the north wind materially diminishes the intertropical heat on the southern coast. The average temperature in October and March, at six o'clock in the morning, is 74° Fahrenheit, and at twelve, in the shade, 81°, and never falls lower than 78°. The average temperature is 75° between eight P. M. and two A. M., and 71° from three to five in the morning.

"The influence of the rainy season also tends to lessen the great heat of the summer. The temperature during the hottest part of the day when it rains does not exceed 81°. At eight o'clock in the morning it maintains itself at 75°, and at three o'clock in the morning it seldom falls as low as 73°. Usually the nights are of almost uniform temperature.

"In summer, when the sky is clear and the sun shines with all its brightness, the thermometer varies between 87° and 90° from eleven in the morning to four in the afternoon. At eight o'clock in the evening it falls to 79°, and at four in the morning to 75°.

"The month of November is the coldest month of the year, and those of May and June the warmest. Towards the close of April, the thermometer, at twelve, in the shade, occasionally ascends to 90°, and rarely descends to 85°. The forepart of the night, on such occasions, maintained itself at 79°, and in the second part the temperature descended to 74°.

"In November the thermometer never falls below 70° from nine to five o'clock in the day; at eight in the evening it never stood at less than 59°, nor less than 55° from four to six in the morning."

The rainy season commences on the Gulf coast about the first of July and ends about the first of November. On that portion of the Isthmus included between the Jaltepec and Sarabia rivers, the rainy season commences about the first of June and ends in December; and at El Barrio it commences about the first of July and ends in October.

These rains are not, however, of sufficient consequence to prevent out-door work for the whole of any one day. The annual fall of rain at Vera Cruz is 66 inches, just one-half the amount which falls in St. Domingo or Jamaica, and even less than that on the northern shores of the Gulf, as at New Orleans or in Florida. It is also considerably less than falls at the Isthmus of Panama.

The altitude of the table lands of Guatimala and Mexico has a more powerful effect in determining the climate of the Isthmus, than what the mere latitude, or its own elevation, could lead to believe. This table land has an average elevation of from 6,500 to 8,200 feet above the sea, which would give a mean temperature of 20° throughout the year less than that of the seaboard: thus, if the temperature of the coast be 85°, that of the table land would be 65°, which is a temperate climate, although within tropical latitudes. This is proved by the growth of oak, cypress, pine, and fern trees, which are inhabitants of a temperate clime; and most of the cerealia of northern latitudes grow in luxuriance. Now, it must be recollected that the Isthmus of Tehuantepec, though in itself possessing only an elevation calculated to lessen the temperature at the sea-board by a few degrees, is subject to the influences of the land in its neighborhood, and its own warmth is very much reduced by the cool air descending from the high table lands and from the Sierra Madre.

At Tehuantepec the rains are of trifling character, and confined to the months of July, August, and September.

The central division of the Isthmus is perhaps the healthiest—a circumstance due to its elevation and better drainage.

Yellow fever has never been known to occur on the Isthmus.

Since the establishment of the Mexican Republic the official returns of the population seem to indicate a sensible decrease—which is at variance with facts. The cause is, that the Indians find it to their advantage to make the returns as small as possible, as, by so doing, many rid themselves of taxes and service in the army of the republic.

Compared with other places selected for forming a junction between the two oceans, this Isthmus has peculiar advantages. With less alluvial land at the sea level, it is more healthy than San Juan de Nicaragua, and from its more northern latitude its mean annual temperature is less than that of Nicaragua or of Panama. The latter place has, indeed, a temperature and climate truly torrid, and partaking more of the character of a continent than of an island, which latter is the peculiarity of the position of this portion of Mexico.

The following is extracted from the Report of the Surgeon to the surveying expedition under P. E. Trastour in 1851:

"It will be seen that the Isthmus of Tehuantepec naturally divides itself into three regions, each different from the other in topography, geological formation, and salubrity.

"The plain of Goatzacoalcos river, flat and low, with an extremely fertile alluvial soil, covered with thick forests, intersected by many rivers, here and there subject to inundation, although the least healthy, yet enjoys a high degree of salubrity, and no fears need be entertained, as proved by the experience of the French emigrants, for those who may in future settle permanently in this region, and much less so for those who may cross it as travelers.

"The region of hills and mountains is as healthy as the most salubrious portions of Europe; full of romantic scenery, it is highly attractive, and will, in progress of time, when inhabited by an enterprising and laborious population, become one of the most beautiful spots on the earth.

"This entire region, for its salubrity, cannot be surpassed by any country whatever. The small villages of Petapa, El Barrio, and Santo Domingo, built on the table land, enjoy a well-merited reputation for uncommon healthiness, not only among the inhabitants of the Isthmus, but many Mexicans come there, even from Oaxaca and several other states of Mexico, to recruit their health.

"Last comes the plain of Tehuantepec, nearly as healthy as the hilly region, although warmer, presenting all the characteristics of a healthy tropical climate.

"All these three regions together form a broad surface of country from the Gulf of Mexico to the coast of the Pacific, of a great variety of resources and of remarkable healthiness, a feature peculiar to the Isthmus, as the lands on both of its sides are very unhealthy; such as Vera Cruz and Tabasco on the Gulf, Acapulco, Huatulco, and the coast of Guatimala on the Pacific shore. This peculiar and exclusive salubrity of the Isthmus, in my opinion, is chiefly due to its configuration, which forms as it were a gate, walled on both sides by heavy masses of mountains, through which pass currents of air that prevail only within the limits of the Isthmus, and render the country they traverse permanently salubrious."

V.

HARBORS.

ATLANTIC PORT.

The superior advantages offered by the mouth of the Goatzacoalcos River as a safe and convenient harbor for ships early attracted the attention of the Spanish conquerors. Cortes, in his official dispatches to the Emperor Charles V., speaks of the importance of this river, as furnishing the best harbor to be found on the Gulf coast of Mexico. In giving the results of a survey of the river made by his order, he says: "They found two fathoms and a half of water at its entrance, in the shallowest part, and ascending twelve leagues, the least they found was five or six fathoms."

These soundings were made in the year 1520, and and give about the same depth over the bar at the mouth of the river which we now find. The fact of there being no delta at the mouth of the river, and the constancy of the depth upon the bar, which has remained unchanged for three centuries, proves that it has attained its "*regimen*," and is not liable to shift or change, a fact which cannot be stated of any other harbor on the coast in the Gulf of Mexico, and indicates that any improvement by deepening the channel may be relied on as permanent. Of the precise character of the formation of this bar many opinions are entertained; and although its position and circumstances seem hardly to justify the conclusion that it is rock, Mr. Temple* has so stated.

The following extract from a letter written by Capt. R. W. Foster, of the steamer "Alabama," who crossed the bar several times, and subsequently sounded it, furnishes some details:

"The extent of the bar east and west is about 220 fathoms, and the breadth, by actual measurement, 108 feet. The bottom, composed of sand and clay, is hard, on which account it is not liable to shift. At high water, on the full and change, the depth is about 13 feet, and falls as low as 11 feet. The general depth, however, is 12 feet, from which in sailing it deepens gradually to five and six fathoms. Except in heavy northers, there is a regular land and sea breeze. The latter sets in between the hours of 9 A. M. and noon.

R. W. Foster.

April, 1851.

"N. B.—The bar, being composed of sand and clay, as already stated, and only 108 feet in width,

* Now Commander Temple, of the U. S. N.

could easily be deepened for vessels of the largest draught to enter."

In view of the testimony, it is presumed that the practicability or security of this harbor will not be questioned. Second, with regard to the capacity of the river itself: Commander Temple reports the head of ship navigation as placed at thirty miles from the mouth, and ten above Minatitlan. By deepening the bar to admit vessels drawing eighteen feet, this depth may be brought without difficulty to Minatitlan, thus forming a secure harbor for nearly thirty miles, along which the track may be laid to any desirable extent.

In reference to the material composing this bar, Commander Temple says that he convinced himself that it was limestone ledge, "with a layer of sand of about four inches deep at the time of our survey, and beneath that was almost everywhere a soft stone. Several loose specimens of pure limestone, and of limestone mixed with clay, were picked up on the beach. I am of opinion that they are a portion of the same ledge. If this be so, it will not only be practicable to deepen the channel over the bar, but the increased depth will remain permanent; for this is the only bar (known to me) on this coast of rock formation, all the others being of shifting sand, sometimes covered with a deposit of mud, although their respective rivers have their origin and course in similar regions with the Goatzacoalcos. It would seem, therefore, that this ledge had been laid bare by the running waters, rather than that it should be the accumulation of ages of deposit. And this appears the more probable, inasmuch as all the local testimony coincides in representing the action of the freshet here to be one of removal instead of, as at the mouth of the Tabasco River, one of deposit, the layer of sand of which mention has been made appearing only when the river is low and the current weak."

PACIFIC PORTS.

The bay of La Ventosa is situated on the southern coast of the Isthmus of Tehuantepec, at twelve miles distance in a southeast direction from the town of that name, and lies between 16° 11′ 36″ and 16° 12′ 49″ north latitude, and 95° 13′ 26″ and 95° 15′ 52″ longitude west from Greenwich, and its western extremity is formed by the Cerro Morro, an isolated rock of oblong shape.

The sandy strand of La Ventosa commences at the foot of the lateral portion of the Cerro Morro, facing the east, and describes from the south to the northeast an arc nearly two miles and a half in length; then takes an easterly and almost rectilinear direction, but drawing a little towards the south, extends on about six miles further, where it runs into the sea; after which it turns back again abruptly and inclines towards the north, though "trending" all the while in an easterly direction.

The sandy beach of La Ventosa itself is cut by lagoons of little depth, having several outlets into the sea, and by the bed of the Tehuantepec River. At the time of the periodical overflow, this current flows over a low country before reaching the Pacific Ocean, in which it then empties itself, not only by its mouth, but also by means of those lagoons, its sole outlets during the dry season.

The volume of the water of the river is subject to very great variations in the course of the year. In the rainy season it reaches twelve feet depth in years of an extraordinary character.

The immense basin of La Ventosa presents a safe and commodious harbor to vessels of all sizes. Closed at the west by the heights of the Morro, it is open at the south and east. This configuration of the bay allows vessels to have ingress and egress irrespective of the quarter from which the wind blows. Throughout its great extent, and on entering it from the sea, no shoals are to be met with; everywhere a good anchorage is to be found. The bottom is of compact sand, and a great proportion of it is mixed with clay.

The depth is almost regularly graduated. It presents at from 350 to 8,000 feet distance from the shore a progressive running from 17 to 53 feet, and averaging for the first thousand feet two feet increase per hundred feet, and about six inches per hundred feet for the following thousand feet.

The greatest difference that has been observed in the level of the water was six and a half feet.

Besides the variable winds, which are rather light, and the land and sea breezes of the morning and evening, two prevalent winds, the north-northeast and south-southwest winds reign during a great portion of the year on the southern coast of the Isthmus. The first of these two atmospheric currents is not felt at sixty miles east of La Ventosa, beyond the Barra de Tonala, nor at sixty-two miles west, beyond the mountain of Chahuhé, which bounds on the west the lagoon of Tengulunda. * * * * *

The north-northeast wind usually begins to blow about the fifteenth of October, and ceases in the forepart of April. In the month of November it blows without interruption, and at that time it reaches its maximum. Towards the middle of December it ceases during intervals of from ten to twelve days, and then begins anew to blow one or two weeks. These alternations or interruptions and renewals are reproduced at short and unequal periods. But the length of the period of discontinuance goes on gradually increasing until the wind only blows one day, and finally ceases completely.

In winter and in summer, during the prevalence of the southerly and northerly winds, the current of the sea is from east to west; its greatest velocity is about one mile and a half per hour. This continual movement in the waters of the Pacific is only discernible at a distance of about 6,000 feet from the shores of La Ventosa.

The bay of La Ventosa is much safer than the harbor of Vera Cruz. Violent tempests frequently render the latter inaccessible during several days, and even when the north wind blows, the communication between the town and the vessels in the harbor is interrupted.

An extract from a letter of Captain Mott, of the steamer "Gold Hunter," which anchored at Ventosa, states as follows. This is dated April 11th, 1851.

"I am much pleased with this port, Ventosa. The holding-ground is excellent, and the depth of six and seven fathoms almost all over the bay very convenient. During the four days we have been here, we have had two fresh southerly winds, and two strong northers. The former did not agitate the sea much, and the latter, though blowing very strong, has not straightened out the chains. We are still riding by the '*bight*,' which is buried in the clay bottom."

Referring again to Commander Temple's report, he says: "From all the foregoing considerations, I am of opinion that La Ventosa is not only the best, but *the* point for a harbor on the Pacific coast of the Isthmus. It is a far safer and better port than either Valparaiso in Chili, or Monterey in California, ports in constant use the year throughout. I speak from personal observation, as well as from an examination of the several charts, and their similarity of outline has suggested the comparison; for, although the indentation of the coast is possibly a little deeper at each of these places than at La Ventosa, yet they are both open to the northward, and as the general 'trend' of the coast is nearly north and south, the prevailing gales blow directly *along* the shore and *into* these harbors, creating a heavy swell, and often forcing vessels to 'slip and go to sea' for safety; whereas at La Ventosa the 'trend' of the coast is east and west, so that the 'northers' blow directly off shore, and create no swell whatever. The danger being from the *sudden* strain brought upon a cable by the surging of a vessel in a sea-way, and not from the steady strain caused by the wind, it follows that northers may be disregarded in an estimate of the safety of this anchorage, as was satisfactorily shown in the case of the Gold Hunter. But northers, although frequent during the winter, and seldom occurring at other seasons, are the only gales that blow in this region. The southerly winds, characteristic of the summer and autumn, are nothing more than thunder squalls of short duration, and incapable of raising a sea. Even the fresh and steady sea breezes that prevailed during the latter portion of our stay at La Ventosa, were unaccompanied by any increase of swell.

"The chart of La Ventosa shows a moderate and almost uniform grade of bottom, beginning with three fathoms at about 100 yards from the beach, and deepening to seven and eight fathoms at a distance of 1,000 yards."

There are few localities where maritime works are not more or less desirable for the protection of vessels against the sea, and at La Ventosa a breakwater forming an inner basin will be desirable ultimately, but the harbor admits at present of daily use without any artificial works, which are only called for in view of extended freighting operations.

VI.

GEOLOGY AND MINERALOGY.

The geological structure of the Isthmus is less clearly marked than that of the adjoining more elevated district of Mexico. Much of the gentle slope of the northern plains is covered over with clay, sand and gravel, and so densely wooded, that no appearance of the rock formation is discernible. The same may be said of the plains on the southern shore. On the middle more elevated regions the conformation is more evident.

The tertiary clays, gravels, and beds of detritus which cover up so much of the Isthmus along the line of survey, extend on the north side almost to the summit-level, and the base of the hills which lie east and west of it. These deposits being found pretty uniformly spread, even to the depth of thirty feet in some places, as at a point north of the summit-level, and between it and the river Almaloya, are evidences of the slow and tranquil elevation of this portion of the Isthmus above the sea, and of its comparatively quiescent condition since a very distant epoch.

Granite and granitiform rocks do not occupy much extent of surface upon the Isthmus, but appears in the higher elevation of the mountain ranges, and in the debris brought down by the rivers.

The prevailing formations is the metamorphic in the various forms attendant upon a granitic nucleus. Slates, primitive limestone and sandstones appear in great variety, and the building stone usually found in this formation are abundant in the hills.

Iron is found in abundance in many points of the Isthmus, and that of Tarifa especially appears to be of excellent quality. The veins of iron ore in the immediate vicinity of San Juan Guichicovi are the richest and most extensive known to exist on the Isthmus. Tin is also found in extremely rich deposits some distance beyond in the Cerro de los Mijes. As regards the precious metals, which made the department of Oajaca once so famous, there is a tradition still prevalent from the time of the conquest that the mountains of Mijes and the upper Uspanapan contain very rich gold and silver mines.

The existence of gold in great quantities in this neighborhood is too well attested, both by tradition and history, to admit of any doubt. The question of its profitable working, however, is a matter yet to be determined.

The following extract shows how over abundant and easily obtained it was at one period upon the Isthmus.

Bernal Diaz, in recording the account of the expeditions of Gonzalo de Umbria and the gold which he brought, says: "Neither did Diego de Ordas, who had been sent to the river Coatzacoalcos, return with empty hands."

Again, in reference to the march of Sandoval: "Twenty of the caziques and principal personages soon made their appearance, bringing with them a present of gold dust in ten tubes, besides various pretty ornaments."

At another place, in the same connection: "We arrived in the province, and began diligently to explore the mines, accompanied by a great number of Indians, who washed the gold dust for us in a kind of trough from the sand of three different rivers. In this way we obtained four tubes full of gold dust, each about the thickness of the middle finger. Sandoval was highly delighted when we brought him these, and concluded that the country must contain rich gold mines,"

"The expedition of Alvarado to Tehuantepec, in 1522, seems to have been attended with far greater success. Bernal Diaz, speaking of this expedition, says: "Among the more powerful tribes who submitted on this occasion, was that of the Tecuantepec (Tzapotecs), whose ambassaders brought with them a present in gold, stating, at the same time, that they were at war with their neighbors, the Tutepecs, who had commenced hostilities with them because they had submitted to the Spanish crown. This tribe inhabited the coast on the South Sea, they added, and possessed great quantities of gold, both in the raw material and in ornaments." Again: "The cazique (of the Tutepecs) soon after arrived with a valuable present in gold, which he repeated almost every day, and provided the troops with abundance of provisions. When Alvarado found what a quantity of gold the inhabitants possessed, he ordered him to make him a pair of stirrups of the finest gold, and gave them a couple of his own for a pattern; and indeed those they made turned out very good."

The same writer, in describing the expedition of Alvarado to this province in the following year, says: "From this place he marched to the large township of Tecuantepec, which is inhabited by a tribe of the Tzapotecs, where he met with the kindest reception, and was presented with some gold dust."

Clavigero, in his history of Mexico, speaking of the abundance of the precious metals in this country, says: "The Mexicans found gold in the countries of the Cohuixcas, the Mixtecas, *Zapotecos*, and in several others. They gathered this precious metal chiefly in grains amongst the sands of the rivers, and the above-mentioned people paid a certain quantity in tribute to the crown of Spain."

The auriferous localities of California are in the alluvial sands and clays, whether they be silicious, aluminous, or basaltic; in granite and primary quartz, and lastly in talcose slate. Although the Sierras of Mexico are a more easterly range, yet their geological constitution is similar to that of California; and it is also on the eastern sides of the range that these metals have been plentifully obtained.

The Andes of South America are the great store-houses of silver for the world. The richness of the mines is almost inconceivable; but their great elevation above the sea makes the climate so cold and the labor of mining so great, as not to be a profitable speculation, except in a few cases.

In Mexico the ores are equally rich; but at a comparatively low elevation, so that where the ore is found in quantity, it is always advantageous to work it.

The general position of silver ores is in veins which traverse the primary and older of the secondary stratified rocks; but especially the former, as well as in the unstratified rocks, the granites and porphyries which accompany the above. In the limestone the silver is generally associated with lead ore, which is then termed argentiferous galena. The same system of rocks which are metalliferous in the other districts of Mexico exist upon the Isthmus; and the limestone contains galena which is argentiferous. An explanation of the metamorphic rocks might lead to the discovery of valuable veins.

That gold exists in the Chivela Pass in considerable quantities, there can be no reasonable doubt. But its discovery is far from being of recent date. It is a well-known fact that the crown on the statue of the Virgin in the church at Chilhuitan is of pure gold, and that it came from the bed of the Rio Verde in the precise locality where the present discoveries have been made. This crown is upwards of fifty years old, and was fabricated at a time when Tehuantepec was a bustling town under the old Spanish regime. Some gold has also been found in the Almaloya; but up to this date a severe day's work has not yielded over three dollar's worth of the precious metal. It occurs in the ferruginous sands in the dry valleys and gorges, but the grains are very small, usually flattened scales, showing that in the original rock it is laminated. Some very fair specimens have been found in fragments of talcose schist, with veins of quartz. This schist is invariably more or less decomposed, and stained with iron rust. The gold thus found in the cellular pockets of the quartoze rock, is associated with copper pyrites, specular iron ore, hematite, &c.

Every one who has passed over the road between Almaloya and the Rio Verde, has been struck with the strong resemblance which the country bears to the metalliferous tracts of Mariposa, and this remark was often made by the California passengers long before any gold was found. The opinion prevails, however, that silver is far more abundant in that locality; and that the rock excavations, which will have to be made through the dividing ridge on the railroad line, will develope veins of incomparable richness. Galena exists almost everywhere in the Chivela Pass; and an antimonial sulphuret of silver occurs here and there with native copper.

It is impossible to say what results may follow a more systematic inspection of the gold fields of the Isthmus. It is undeniable, however, that the operation of mining will be expensive, and it is this fact which has thus far discouraged explorations.

The hills of San Martin, on the Gulf towards the west, are of a volcanic character, and contain cinnabar ore in abundance. From this mineral (the sulphuret of mercury) almost all the quicksilver of commerce is made. Its location here is a future source of riches to the Isthmus.

Petroleum abounds in this neighborhood on the banks of the Goatzacoalcos in quantities, and conveniently disposed for shipping.

With reference to the energy of the present volcanic action in the country, everything on the Isthmus bears the mark of stability, and the absence of any active volcanic force. This is a point of great importance where the stability and permanence of large buildings are concerned; and in this respect, this portion of Mexico is less liable to motions of the ground than Guatimala or Nicaragua; in which latter place several alterations of level have taken place lately.

Previous absence of upheaval and eruption through a long period of time is *a priori* evidence of the non-existence of the upheaving cause; and this is the actual condition of the Isthmus of Tehuantepec.

VII.

TIMBER AND VEGETABLE PRODUCTIONS.

On all the rivers of the Isthmus are seen huge specimens of the most valuable trees of the equinoctial regions; amongst the many valuable woods, is the Encina (live oak,) which grows in great profusion.

Remote from the river margins, the limit of the periodic overflow is marked by the presence of many varieties of trees of great value, as the *mahogany*, the *cedro*, varieties of the oak, the ebony, the iron wood, the *lignum-vitæ*, "chico-zapote," "quiebra-hacha," or "break axe," and the "acacia." In a pecuniary point of view the value of these products is immeasurable, especially that which would result from the felling of mahogany and cedar alone. As we ascend the rivers, first appears the oak, then the pines which grow to an enormous size. Indeed, the abundance of these and other building timber of equivalent value, is such that the only limit which can be assigned to the supply they may yield is the demand for centuries to come.

Not less important in value, perhaps, is the india-rubber tree, which is found in astonishing numbers throughout the forests that skirt the tributary streams. Its value, however, is so little appreciated there, that the gum is only gathered for foot-balls, or for some medicinal purposes.

So far as the necessary purposes of construction are concerned, there will be found no lack of durable timber on the Isthmus. Among these we may enum-crate the guapaque. In the Parroquia, at Tehuantepec, built by Cocijopi, last cacique of the Zapotecos, in 1530, the staircase is made of guapaque, which to to this time exhibits no evidence of decay. Another instance of the durability of this valuable wood occurs at Boca del Monte, in the uprights of a little chapel, which have been buried in the ground for more than twenty-five years, and are still sound and perfect. In the construction of the Vera Cruz railroad, the cross-ties and sleepers are made of guapaque, and, notwithstanding the exposed condition of the superstructure, the wood remains unchanged. Both mahogany and cedar are lasting timbers, as is satisfactorily proved by the age of the canoes, many of which are known to be more than forty years old. Of the value of the pine, oak, and cypress, it is, perhaps, sufficient to say that there are many of these trees (felled by the Spaniards) in a more or less perfect state of preservation, still lying in the Rio del Corte, where they serve to recall the faded glory of the naval arsenal at Havana. The castarica is also a valuable building timber, which possesses the merit of being indestructible by insects; and the macaya seems particularly adapted for the purposes of hydraulic construction. The javicue, or jabi, also merits attention for its exceeding hardness and durability. This wood is incorruptible in water, and is useful for naval construction.

Of the maize, frijoles, sugar, cacao, tobacco, coffee, and cotton raised on the Isthmus, it is difficult to speak in terms which might convey an adequate idea of the adaptation of the soil and climate to their cultivation, or the perfection to which they are susceptible of being brought.

This is the native country of maize, and, upon the wet land, *milpas* (those subject to periodic overflow,) the yield is two crops annually, each of which averages sixty bushels to the acre, and without other labor than the mere planting. Indeed, it is no uncommon sight to see the reaper and the sower in the same field.

The fecundity of the Mexican variety of maize is astonishing. Fertile lands usually afford a return of three or four hundred fold. The general estimate for the Ishmus may be considered as one hundred and fifty fold.

The sugar-cane, though cultivated to a limited extent, except on one or two plantations, is, nevertheless, of astonishing magnitude and richness; the stalks not unfrequently exhibiting *twenty-eight* joints, with a diameter ranging from two to three inches. It is even found growing wild in the valleys and *potreros*, and of a quality and luxuriance (according to Tadeo Ortiz) superior to that of the Antilles.

In the hands of an efficient planter, and with other care than the mere bounty of nature, it is not difficult to conceive the perfection and value to which the sugar-cane of the Isthmus might be brought, especially when we consider the adaptation of the soil and climate to its cultivation, the facilities of transporting it across the plains to the ports of the Pacific, and the close proximity of the markets of California.

The pita or ixtle grows everywhere on the Atlantic Plains of the Isthmus. This plant, which is a species of hemp, produces a textile thread far superior in strength, length, and fineness of fibre to the best vegetable productions of China; but, owing to the absence of machinery, this prolific plant is indifferently and imperfectly manufactured, or prepared as a raw material. The small quantity produced by hand labor, is sent into the interior of Mexico and there woven with other materials into cloth, which is extensively used in clothing. The fibre of this plant often measures two feet in length. For cordage and small ropes it is superior to the hemp of Sisal, and for the manufacture of paper it has no superior. It requires no labor for its cultivation, and is as easily gathered and baled as hay. It grows over so vast an extent of country, that in view of the extensive demand for paper stock, it could be made the source of immense revenue.

Of the cacao, the growth of which is spontaneous, one variety called "petaste" has a delightful aromatic flavor, and is greatly esteemed. The quality is said to be superior to that of Guayaquil or Maracaibo, and the prolific return which characterizes its cultivation is sure evidence of its importance and value. The lands east of the Goatzacoalcos seem particularly adapted to its growth.

The plantations of tobacco are both numerous and considerable, especially in the northern and central divisions of the Isthmus. That raised in the Chimalapas and on the uplands generally, is known by the name of "tabaco del monte." This variety is powerfully narcotic, coarse, and grows to a large size, the leaves averaging *thirty-three* inches in length, and *fifteen* in breadth. Another kind, cultivated on the plains, and called "corral," is smaller, and of a flavor and quality which is said to be superior to the best *vuelta de abajo* of Cuba. It is only necessary to say that the soil is admirably adapted to it, and it can be grown equally well in all parts.

The land east of the Goatzacoalcos, and that which skirts the Mexican Gulf, is characterized by the abundance of allspice (*myrtus pimenta*) disseminated over its surface. Near Ventosa, on the Pacific plains, the cassia-tree is plentiful, but the only use made of it is for occasional purposes of construction.

The banks of the Goatzacoalcos exhibit, in a wild state, the greatest abundance of *coffee*, and, with few exceptions, no pains are taken to cultivate it, although the quality is admitted to be very superior. This neglect may be readily accounted for in the universal preference which exists among the natives for chocolate.

The amount of *rice* cultivated on the Isthmus, compared with the quantity the land is susceptible of yielding, is exceedingly insignificant; but in the potreros, between the Goatzacoalcos and Tonala rivers, the plantations are of considerable value. That which most particularly characterizes this region, is the singular fact, that one single sowing of rice will yield successively two large crops without the slightest additional labor.

The *cotton* plantations of the Isthmus are so trifling as scarcely to deserve the name, but the fitness of the soil and climate to produce it are beyond question. There are two varieties, one of which, raised in the neighborhood of Minatitlan, is not inferior in texture, whiteness, or length of staple, to the finest uplands of the Southern United States. With the single exception of Acayucan, there are no gins in the country, and as the seed is, therefore, separated by hand, (a work which is tedious and protracted,) the cultivation of cotton in other parts is necessarily small. What would seem to favor the cultivation of cotton, is the sheltered condition of the table lands and savannas, and the entire absence of the *army worm*, which so seriously damages the cotton crops of the Southern States. It is entirely unknown to the natives.

The enumeration of all the vegetable dyes found on the Isthmus, with all that might be said of the numerous varieties, would constitute matter for a well filled volume on botany, rather than the general details of a statistical report. The indigo plant grows spontaneously in the wildest profusion, and is gathered in the rude method of the natives for their own use, and, when it is recollected that the European consumption of this dye amounts to some 28.000.000 lbs. yearly, the value of this product alone may be realized.

The growth of Brazil wood and logwood is so great in every part of the Isthmus, that they call for special notice of the fact.

In a commercial point of view, the vegetable gums and balsams are items of important consideration. In the central and southern districts, the abundance of the balsam of Peru, and a bark which serves in treatment as a substitute for quinine, is astonishing. Not less worthy of note is the *styrax officinale* of Linnæus, the product of which is known as the liquid amber gum; and the numerous varieties of acacia furnish gum arabic in the greatest profusion.

The medicinal plants of the Isthmus present an innumerable variety, as the liquorice root, the sarsaparilla, and vanilla; the *laurus-sassafras*, the *cubeba canina*, and many others. The superior quality of the vanilla and sarsaparilla, found in almost every point of the Isthmus, and their incredible profusion of growth, cannot fail to prove a source of the most lucrative trade. Already the inhabitants cultivate them to some extent; but the amount under culture bears no comparison to that which grows wild in the dense forests.

In the production of fruits and leguminous plants, the Isthmus, perhaps, stands unrivaled. Many of them claim particular notice, either for their delicious flavor, abundant growth, or the nutritive qualities for which they are distinguished: among these we find the chicozapote, limoncillo, orange, chayote, cocoanut, lemon, pineapple (sometimes reaching the enormous weight of fifteen pounds), melon, mamey, chiraymoya, citron, mango, banana, plantain, guava, and pomegranate.

When we reflect upon the productiveness of the soil, the salubrity of the climate, and the boundless character of the vegetation of the Isthmus, it is not difficult to see how great must be the reward which would crown the efforts of an industrious planter.

VIII.

ANIMALS.

THE fauna of the Isthmus presents a rich and boundless field both for the realization of pecuniary results, and for scientific investigation; but it is a subject which commands but little attention beyond the point at which it interests by ministering to the daily wants of the traveler or the operative, and therefore we shall confine ourselves to a bare recital of the more useful animals.

The domestic animals at present found on the Isthmus are, with rare exceptions, not indigenous, but were introduced from Europe in the sixteenth century, or at periods subsequent to the conquest of the country by the Spaniards. Some of these have since multiplied to a surprising extent, particularly horses, mules, and cattle, which are found in the greatest numbers throughout the inhabited parts.

The immense potreros, which border all the principal streams on the northern division, furnish rich pastures of never-failing verdure for numerous herds. During the short season that these potreros are inundated, the cattle are driven to the more elevated savannas, remote from the river margins. The extensive table lands in the central portions of the Isthmus, as well as the plains bordering the Pacific, also furnish abundance of excellent pasturage. Indeed, the whole country seems peculiarly well adapted to the raising of horned cattle. With little care on the part of their owners, they increase rapidly, grow to a large size, and have a remarkably sleek and well-favored appearance. Enjoying a range of the finest pastures in the world, they are usually in good condition, and make fair beef. The inhabitants make very little use either of the flesh or the hides of their cattle; and milk is a luxury seldom enjoyed. This is a trait of the Indian character, to have forgotten, if it had ever known, the use of milk.

On some of the estates it is not uncommon to find five, ten, or even twenty thousand head of cattle, many of which roam over the prairies in a wild state, and when required for beef, or any other purpose, are secured by means of the *lasso*.

No attention is paid to the breeding of cattle, as little value is set upon them; and the proprietor of the hacienda is often as poor amid his herds, as the peon whose life is spent in their care. But, when the resources of the Isthmus shall have been developed by the establishment of proper roads, markets, and means of transport and communication, the immense droves which now roam wild in various localities will be found to constitute an important element of wealth.

The horses found in this portion of Mexico are of small size, and almost uniformly poor in flesh. They are, however, of great endurance, and possess much more spirit than is indicated in their looks. Comparatively, they are very intelligent, and under the guidance of the powerful Mexican bit are easily managed. The inhabitants employ them principally as saddle-beasts, though sometimes for draught, in which case the load is invariably attached to the animal's tail. As ridiculous and barbarous as this custom may appear, it is said to cause the horse no pain; and if one may judge by the weight of the load, and the quiet manner in which the animal submits to the practice, this would seem to be the case. At all events, this primitive application of power is worth an engineer's remembrance, and may serve a useful purpose in some necessary contingency. But a small portion of the horses are broke to use, the greater number being allowed to run untrained on the prairies.

Nearly the entire transportation of the country is carried on by means of mules, which are small but very hardy, and peculiarly well adapted to the rough roads found in the more elevated sections. Their usual load is 225 lbs., but on the plains they often carry from 400 to 500.

In the prosecution of such works as may be required for the opening of a line of communication across the Isthmus, the advantages accruing from the great number of horses, mules and cattle can hardly be overrated. Good beeves may be had at prices ranging from four to six dollars per head; and for purposes of draught there is no lack of oxen. On the Pacific plains, where the surface of the country is sufficiently level to admit of wheeled vehicles, they are extensively employed—the yoke being secured by hide thongs to the horns.

Deer are found in great multitudes in all sections, and serve as an abundant source of prey for the numerous voracious animals which infest the country.

The inhabitants make but little use either of the skins or furs of the wild animals found here, though many of them are of considerable value.

It has been truly observed, that as Africa is the country of beasts, so Mexico is the country of birds. This is especially true of the southern provinces; and among the almost endless varieties peculiar to the Isthmus, a large proportion of them are valuable either for the food they furnish, the beautiful plumage in which they are decked, or the sweet songs they pour forth.

An important class of birds in the Isthmus, such as the Wild Turkey, Crested Curassow, Partridge, *Chachalaca*, Tinamou, Quail, Pigeon, and Dove, are found in great abundance through all parts of the country. The Crested Curassow is a magnificent game-bird: it approaches the Turkey in size, and is easily domesticated, when it becomes very tame.

In the dense forests which skirt the Jaltepec River on the south, both the Wild Turkey and Curassow are surprisingly numerous, and have so little fear of man that the Indians frequently kill them by means of stones or other missiles. The *Chachalaca* is about the size of a common fowl, and its flesh is even more delicate and nutritious.

It will be seen from this hasty glance at the birds of the Isthmus, that this country presents a rich field for the investigations of the ornithologist; and it is to those professionally skilled in this branch of zoology that we must leave the enumeration and detailed description of the immense variety of birds inhabiting it.

Excellent fish are found in great profusion in all the rivers and arroyos that drain the slopes of the Cordillera, particularly in the smaller streams. In most of the larger ones there are many varieties of good size and fine quality; indeed, fish constitutes an important item of food for the inhabitants. Those living at Santa Maria Chimalapa, having but few domestic animals and no means of killing game, subsist almost entirely upon the fish obtained from the Rio del Corte. These are taken in such numbers that they are salted and transported to supply the towns of the central division. Indeed there is, perhaps, no country in the world, situate within the same parallels of latitude, that produces an equivalent quantity and variety of fish and wild game as the Isthmus.

IX.

TOWNS, PRODUCTIVE INDUSTRY, ETC.

The towns which are scattered over the Isthmus present so many interesting features, and are so intimately connected with the establishment of a great commercial route, that they deserve a passing notice. Their situation, the character of their inhabitants, the nature of the lands within their jurisdiction, and the productive industry of various localities, are all matters of importance to the construction of a railroad, and to the future colonization and destinies of the Isthmus. We can notice but a few of the most important on the line of the proposed road, and these but briefly.

Minatitlan claims attention, not only from its being the present head of ship navigation on the Goatzacoalcos, but also as the only existing outlet on the north for the surplus productions of the Isthmus. The village is located on the western bank of the river, twenty miles from its mouth, with a mixed population who are variously occupied as boatmen, agriculturists, and carpenters. Back of the village, the land continues moderately high and undulating for some distance, but the river margins in the immediate proximity are low and subject to periodic inundation. Timber of all kinds grows in great abundance, and the profusion of fruit, as guavas, oranges, mangoes, melons, lemons, &c., is not the least interesting feature of the place. The people generally are more intelligent than in other towns of the Isthmus, a fact which is doubtless due to their intercourse with foreigners. The climate is generally salubrious and healthy; and the advantageous position of the village, its limited distance from the sea, and the capacity of the river at that point for ship navigation, cannot fail, under any circumstances, to make it hereafter a place of considerable importance.

Eight miles westerly from Minatitlan is the village of San Juan Chinameca, beautifully located on an abrupt alluvial spur, the sides of which slope to the north, east, and south. It contains well-constructed houses, with balconies supported by arches of stone. The principal object of interest in the village is the church, built in the centre of a beautiful common, surrounded by lofty cocoanut-trees running parallel to the sides of the building, which is an oblong stone structure with arched doorways and tiled roof. The interior decorations, though rudely made, are nevertheless valuable, especially the candlesticks and altar service, which are formed of silver said to have been brought from the head-waters of the Uspanapa. Chinameca contains about 1,400 inhabitants, who are characterized by industrious habits and hospitality. The houses, which are chiefly *adobe*, are ranged to face the sides of a long, winding street, forming quite a contrast with the mud ranchos of neighboring villages. In the vicinity are several fine estates, containing in the aggregate some 5,000 head of horned cattle, and upwards of 1,200 horses and mules. At a distance of two leagues from Chinameca is a coffee plantation, growing 7,000 trees, and within six miles of the village, in the direction of San Martin, is a spring of thermal water.

JALTIPAN, reached by an excellent mule-road five miles southwesterly from the last mentioned village, is somewhat celebrated as being the birth-place of the romantic and seductive *Malinche*, or *Doña Marina*, the favored mistress of Hernan Cortes. The town, which has a population of 2,300, and some 400 houses huddled together without reference to order or regularity, with the exception of one or two principal streets, is laid on a slightly elevated plain, which overlooks the contiguous country. At the southern end of the town is an extensive artificial mound, about 40 feet in height by 100 in diameter at the base, known as the "Hill of Malinche." The inhabitants raise considerable indian-corn, sugar-cane, tobacco, and ixtle. The island of Tacamichapa is reputed to belong to the town, and is claimed on the ground that it was conceded to Malinche by the crown of Spain, in consideration of the invaluable services rendered by her to the great conqueror. The women of this place are not undeservedly famed as the fairest and most beautiful throughout the district; and in times past are said to have carried their ideas of hospitality and entertainment to a very singular degree.

Mr. Moro says: "A singular circumstance, deserving the attention of the ethnologist, is the existence of a race of *dumb* people, of which there are numerous families in Jaltipan. However strange this may appear, it is nevertheless certain, and the *Rancho de los Mudos*, established a few years since, near the lower part of the island of Tacamichapa, owes its designation to the fact that the individuals are all dumb who inhabit the settlement."

Jaltipan enjoys a great salubrity; fevers are seldom known to occur, and the musquitoes and other annoying insects are exceedingly few.

Nine miles southwest from Jaltipan is TESISTEPEC, built on the summit of a broken sandstone ridge, and contains a population of 2,200, who are almost entirely Indians. The town is supplied with water from wells, sunk in the rock to depths varying from 20 to 40 feet. The soil in this vicinity is remarkably fertile, and tobacco, rice, maize, sugar-cane and ixtle are produced in large quantities. The principal manufactures of Tesistepec are shoes and cigars. The neighborhood abounds with excellent cattle. The numerous metallic indications of this locality invest it with peculiar interest.

SAN MARTIN ACAYUCAN is the most important town in the northern division of the Isthmus, and the capital of the district of the same name. Located on a ridge which extends from the mountains of Tuxtla, its climate is cool, salubrious, and healthy. It is the residence of the *gefe politico*, and a place of considerable trade, containing some 5,200 inhabitants, a parroquia, two or three primary schools, several stores, a cotton-gin, and one or two sugar-presses. Latterly, however, Acayucan has greatly diminished in wealth and importance. At the period of the Conquest it was the court and residence of one of the most powerful caciques of the great empire of the Aztecs; but, unfortunately, the old archives have perished with its greatness, and a few incomplete documents recording the events of the years 1600 and 1658 are all that now remain. In the vicinity the soil is remarkably fertile, producing maize, sugar-cane, coffee, cacao, ixtle, and a great variety of esculents. The surrounding forests also abound with valuable trees. Most of the trade of Acayucan is carried on through the Paso San Juan, on the river of that name, which serves as an outlet for the productions of all the northern division, except such as find a market by sea from Minatitlan. In times of prosperity the annual exports of cotton and ixtle alone, through the Paso, to Vera Cruz are said to have reached beyond $1,256,000.

Within the jurisdiction of the town are numerous haciendas and settlements, abounding in cattle, horses, and mules, and presenting many features of interest to the agriculturist by the fecundity of the soil; to the machinist, by the abundant sources of water-power; to the sportsman, by the myriads of game; to the geologist, by the nature and variety of the formations; to the botanist, by the rich and varied character of the vegetation; to the antiquarian, by the number of ancient idols and relics; and to the ethnologist, by the heterogeneous condition of the people.

After leaving Acayucan, there are not any settlements met with throughout all the broad belt of country lying contiguous to the Goatzacoalcos, until reaching MAL PASO, otherwise called the *Paso del Sarabia*, situated at the forks of the Goatzacoalcos and Sarabia rivers, and the present general head of canoe navigation for all travel to and from the northern and southern division of the Isthmus. The products of the Pacific side, destined for the Gulf coast, are first brought down to this place for embarkation; and occasional cargoes of goods from Vera Cruz ascend the river to this point, from whence they are carried to the Pacific plains on mules.

Beyond Mal Paso is SAN GABRIEL BOCA DEL MONTE (entrance to the forest). This is an extensive hacienda, between the Sarabia and Malatengo rivers, and is traversed by the road which connects the more interior towns with Mal Paso and the Goatzacoalcos. The road for the whole distance (to within a mile of the hacienda) lies through a dense forest, that scarcely permits the rays of the sun to penetrate. On emerging from the forest, the view of the surrounding country is extremely beautiful; and by ascending a small eminence, immense prairies, clothed with luxuriant grass, are seen stretching to the bases of the distant mountains. Looking south, one sees the low depression formed by the passes through the dividing ridge which separates the waters of the two oceans; and to the right and left the main chain of the great Cordillera, rising in sublime grandeur. The soil, with the exception of that in the valley, and on the margins of the streams, is coarse, gravelly, and unproductive: this refers especially to the country south and west of the Hacienda. To the north the vegetation is more rank, and the character of the land superior. The number of cattle about Boca del Monte is limited to less than 3,000, but they are remarkably well-conditioned, and generally a larger breed than are found on the Atlantic plains.

Southwesterly, nine miles from this Hacienda, is the extensive Indian pueblo of San Juan Guichicovi, accessible by a narrow mule-road, which crosses the Mogañe (one of the tributaries of the Malatengo) five miles from Boca del Monte. The inhabitants, who constitute the remnant of the old Mije tribe, are generally an idle, worthless set, half civilized, and poor amid abundant sources of wealth. Their number is about 5,200, who cultivate the rich valley and bottom lands to some extent, raising maize, sugar-cane, ixtle, rice, frijoles, and plantains. The number of cattle is comparatively small, but the inhabitants pride themselves on the possession of their mules, which are said to amount to several thousand. The chief object of interest at San Juan Guichicovi is its venerable church, which is an unfinished stone structure, oblong, with broken arches, roofless, and in ruins. Of the date of its foundation nothing is now known.

With the exception of Espiritu Santo, Santa Maria Petapa, about ten miles south of this is the oldest Spanish settlement on the Isthmus, and is prettily located on a plain, bounded on the north and west by an amphitheatre of lofty mountains. This town, which once contained a population of 5,000, is now reduced to a little more than 1,300, who raise maize, frijoles, indigo, calabashes, limes, &c. The church, still in a very perfect state, is said to be upwards of 300 years old. This is a rectangular building, about 200 feet by 50, with a low dome, and constructed after the style of the sixteenth century. It contains a tolerable organ and some very good paintings, among which that of the "Annunciation" and the "Prayer in the Garden" are best. The walls are indifferently painted in stucco, and the images present some rude specimens of carving. Within the last half century, Petapa has dwindled to an insignificant village; and a few agricultural products, and some manufactured articles, as shoes and buckskins, constitute the only resources of the people.

El Barrio de la Soledad on the road to Tehuantepec within two miles of Petapa, contains a mixed population composed of Indians and Zambos. The town has a well built church, and in the neighborhood are some fine estates upon which a considerable quantity of cane is grown.

Immediately east and south of El Barrio are a number of small settlements embraced within the limits of the estates of Marquesanas: these include *La Chivela*, *Tarifa*, *Santiago*, and *Agua Escondida*. The hacienda of *La Chivela*, situated on the plains, at the entrance of the pass of the same name, 780 feet above the Pacific Ocean, and twelve miles southeasterly from Petapa, is only important as being the residence of the chief *guarda de ganado* of the "Marquesanas," the property of Don Estevan Maqueo, and the principal place for the sale of cattle belonging to the estate.

Santiago, beautifully located on a level plain, seven miles from La Chivela, and three miles from the Pass, is surrounded by an amphitheatre of hills. Its elevation is 800 feet above the Pacific, and the *Wine-palm* grows in great abundance all throughout its vicinity.

Tarifa, built on the plains of that name, derives some interest from its being the point selected by Señor Moro for the western termination of his ship-canal feeder, which was to conduct the waters of the Chicapa and Ostuta rivers along the southern slope of the Albricia range to the summit level of these plains. It is possible that the waters of the Rio del Corte might be brought to Tarifa on a shorter distance, at a much less cost, and a more abundant supply obtained. But little doubt, however, exists that from either of these sources a sufficiency of water for the summit-level of a ship-canal, with capacity to pass 100 ships per day, might be brought. The item of *cost* would, therefore, determine the source and the route of the feeder.

San Miguel Chimalapa is built in the valley of the Chicapa River at its confluence with the Monetza. This town, which is inhabited exclusively by Indians of the Zoque tribe (of whom only about three-fourths speak Spanish), has a population of 460, who are chiefly occupied in raising *ixtle*, from the manufactures of which considerable trade is carried on with Juchitan and Tehuantepec. Timber of all kinds is particularly abundant about this vicinity; and there are many valuable sites for mills on the Chicapa.

Between San Miguel and Santa Maria Chimalapa the road is, perhaps, the most rugged on the Isthmus, and for the greater part of the distance (nine leagues) lies through a dense and almost impenetrable forest, traversed by inumerable small streams, which, during the rainy months, are so swollen as to be impassable. Four leagues beyond this is the beautiful Cerro *Jacal de Ocotal*, so called from the ocote (or pine) forest which covers its summit. From this point the view of the country is magnificent, and the hues of the foliage from every conceivable form and variety of tree in the valleys beneath, surpass in richness the most brilliant tints of our northern Indian summer.

The town of Santa Maria Chimalapa is built with some regularity on an elevated ridge, within a mile of the Rio del Corte, and contains 2 churches, 104 houses, and a population of 680, of whom no more than three-fourths speak Spanish. Distant from the shores of the Pacific, and approachable only by a wretched road, the inhabitants have comparatively little social intercourse with other settlements. Their products are nevertheless much more numerous than those of more favored places, and considerable quantities of oranges, maize, tobacco and ixtle are annually transported by means of *balsas* down the Rio del Corte, for the supply of El Barrio, Petapa, &c. The river abounds in excellent fish, and the inhabitants, whose cattle, from the want of grazing lands, are very limited, eat scarcely any other animal food. The scenery on the Rio del Corte is unequaled in beauty, and the abundance of valuable timber, as the pine, live-oak, and cypress, invest this part with peculiar interest, and cannot fail to attract a share of the future timber trade of the Isthmus.

Returning again to the central division of the Isthmus, the road from Petapa to Tehuantepeć takes a direction nearly south, by the way of the Cerro Guié-vixia, and through the Pass of Guichilona. Near here is a branch road leading to San Geronimo, a league from the mountain bases, on the margin of the Rio Juchitan. This town, founded by the Spaniards soon after the Conquest, contains a population of 500 Zapotecos, whose chief occupation is the raising of indigo. With the exception of its admirable situation and healthy climate, the only attraction is the church, built by the Dominican friars in the sixteenth century. This is an oblong edifice, in the Moorish style of architecture, and in very good repair, considering the carelessness of the natives, and the long period of years that have intervened since its erection. Above the altar there are some tolerable *basso relievo* carvings of the patron saints of the pueblo—of San Miguel, San Pablo, and San Elias. Altogether, the village is neat and picturesque. The railroad will probably pass through it or in its vicinity.

Leading to San Geronimo is a road from Chivela Pass, a portion of which was built by the engineers of Don José de Garay. In some places this is quite steep, and presents many difficulties for wheeled vehicles; but by blasting at one or two points it may be rendered almost immediately serviceable. All along the line through the Pass the scenery is beautifully varied, and within a short distance of the plains are several mineral springs, which with so many attractive features are doubtless destined to become places of frequent resort. Indeed, it is not unlikely that the Springs of Chivela may become, in the course of time, as well known and as fashionably frequented as those of *Saratoga* and the *White Sulphur*. After reaching the base of the mountains in the vicinity of the Rio Verde, the road finally comes on to the plains through the Portillo de la Martar.

Two miles northwest from San Geronimo is the neat settlement of Santo Domingo Chihuitan, through the centre of which courses the clear, silvery stream of Los Perros. Beyond a picturesque location and its beautiful church, Chihuitan is an unimportant place, numbering some 600 inhabitants, who are remarkable for their hospitality; it is, however, the chosen resort of thousands who congregate from all portions of the Isthmus to attend a fair annually held there. This generally lasts for a week, during which time the roads in every direction are thronged by the Indians, who hail the occasion to expose for sale, at so grand a market, the trifling results of their industry.

Almost directly south from San Geronimo, at a distance of five miles, is the town of Itztaltepec, signifying in the Zapoteco language "the Hill of Salt." The town contains an industrious and quiet population of 1,500; and the number of well-built houses, cisterns, indigo-vats, and other stone structures, attest the vanished thrift and prosperity of the place.

With the exception of Tehuantepec, JUCHITAN, five miles south of the last named village, is the largest town on the southern division of the Isthmus, and contains a population of nearly 6,000, among whom are many Europeans. Of the foundation of this place little or nothing is now known, although tradition imputes to it a very great antiquity. Its appearance from the plains on the north is that of a large city, and the contrast between the white of its buildings and the deep brilliant hues of the surrounding foliage is pleasing to the utmost. Somewhat conspicuous, in the central part of the town, is the Parroquia, built by the Dominican friars in the early part of 1600: this is an antique looking structure with arched roof and massive walls, supported at the corners by strong buttresses, which are surmounted by columned towers and pinnacles. The chancel consists of massive carvings in gilt, and the interior walls are variously painted in stucco. On each side, above the altar table, are very well executed pictures of the apostles Peter and Paul, and in the centre is an excellent painting of San Vicente, the patron saint of the town. The whole structure is inclosed by a brick wall several feet in thickness, with high arched gateways opening on the south and east.

The inhabitants of Juchitan are characterized by habits of industry, and their numerous manufactures of hats, shoes, cotton cloth, hides, buckskins, mats, hammocks, &c., bear ample testimony to their mental superiority over the other settlements of the Isthmus. Among the articles raised are maize, indigo, and fruits. In addition, considerable valuable wood is annually gathered, and the inhabitants export large quantities of tallow and gum arabic. Altogether, and in spite of many severe obstacles imposed by the government, Juchitan is the most industrious and thrifty town on the Pacific plains. Its appearace is enlivened by bustling shops, and the streets are more or less filled with ponderous carts drawn by oxen, and laden either with salt from the lagoons, or goods brought from Guatimala.

Tehuantepec is the second town in the State of Oaxaca in point of numbers, manufacturing and commercial importance. It is situated eleven miles from the Bay of Ventosa, and about the same distance from Salina Cruz. It contains a population of about 13,000 inhabitants, mostly Indians, some half breeds, and a few Castilians. The better class are very aristocratic, the half breeds civil and polite, the poor Indians humble and thankful for the smallest favor. Tehuantepec boasts of sixteen churches, among which is the venerable Parroquia built by Cocijopi, last cacique of the Zapotecos, in the year 1530, when it was dedicated to the purposes of Christian worship by the Dominican friars, to whom it was left as a legacy by the ill-used and dying cacique. Its massive walls, arched gateways, and ruined dome, though fast crumbling to decay, speak in voiceless eloquence of the greatness of a people whose dust is mingled with its own.

The manufactured articles of Tehuantepec are leather, cotton cloth, silken sashes, shoes, hats, mats, silver-ware, saddles, horse appointments, and pottery, besides a considerable quantity of buckskins and soap. The department of Tehuantepec is controlled by a governor, who exercises jurisdiction over all the alcaldes of all the towns and barrios, and who is directly responsible to the State government at Oaxaca. Police duty is performed by the soldiers of the National Guard, whose quarters command the entrance to the plaza. The trade with Oaxaca consists of cochineal, cacao, fish, *camarones*, saddles, shoes, and leather; with Guatimala (which is *contraband*) it is mostly manufactured English and French goods, as calicoes, linen, muslin, silk and cotton handkerchiefs.

The *coup d'œil* from the summit of the Cerro del

Tigre is pleasing and picturesque in the greatest degree. But age, decay, war, and a hundred untold calamities have swept away the city's greatness, and everything now wears the gray and grief-worn aspect of olden days. The houses are of massive structure, like antique fortresses, and of a style that might have rivaled those of more classic lands. But where once was wealth, and hope, and comfort, the spider now weaves his web. Westward the Tehuantepec River is visible, clear, and winding through many a league, its banks margined with fields of grain and the houses of old aristocratic landholders. Westward, further still, is the mountain of Guiéngola, with its ruined city, its broken arches and crumbling columns. Looking south, lies Ventosa and the granite hills of the Morro dividing it from Salina Cruz. There are plains here, there, and everywhere, watered by many a stream, clothed with luxuriant woods, decked with fields, ripe and in blossom, and smiling with an eternal spring-like beauty. On the opposite shore is San Sebastian and San Blas, the pictures of quietude, ruin, and decay; and beneath, noisy men, marching soldiers, beseeching beggars, laden mules, braying asses, and dark, voluptuous women. But, besides all these, Tehuantepec has her public schools, play-grounds, flower-gardens, and places of amusement, stores, cabinet shops, shoemakers' shops, and workers in silver, brass, iron, and other metals. There are also several hotels and *posadas* for the accommodation of travelers.

Immediately south and in close proximity to Ventosa is a broad rich plain, which offers incomparable advantages for the location of a city. Free from overflow, or the presence of miasmatic marshes, and with abundant sources of delightful water on either side, it is but reasonable to conclude that before many years the dense forest which now studs the plain will give place to cheerful habitations, and that where now only is the abode of the bird and the insect will be heard the hum and the bustle of life's business.

X.

SOURCES OF REVENUE.

If we look at the map of the American Continent, it will be seen that the Isthmus of Tehuantepec is the most favorable point at which an inter-oceanic communication can be established, whether we consider it in reference to the United States alone, or to the American, European, and Asiatic countries. From Europe or the United States to the Pacific it is the *shortest* route of any, either now in operation, or that is at present contemplated, with the exception of the Union Pacific R. R. now just completed. This is clearly exhibited by the following table, showing the respective distances from England, New York and New Orleans, to the port of San Francisco, in California, by the routes of Panama, and *Tehuantepec*, compared with the voyages from the same places round Cape Horn, and showing the distances each would respectively save by traversing the American Isthmus. The various Isthmian transits intermediate between Panama and Tehuantepec are of no interest in this connection.

Voyage to San Francisco, in California.	Round Cape Horn.	*Via* Panama.	*Via* Tehuantepec	Difference in favor of Tehuantepec.
	Miles.	Miles.	Miles.	Miles.
From England (Liverpool)	15,710	8,607	7,476	1,131
From New York..........	16,360	6,218	4,741	1,477
From New Orleans.........	16,500	5,718	3,384	2,334
		Distance saved *via* Panama.	Distance saved *via* Tehuantepec	
Saved by England.........		7,103	8,234	1,131
" by New York........		10,142	11,619	1,477
" by New Orleans.....		10,782	13,116	2,334

The shortest line between England and Sidney, in Australia, lies through the Isthmus of Tehuantepec.

The Tehuantepec route is, of all the routes proposed from the Atlantic to the Pacific Ocean, the true American route. It is the route which is entirely commanded by our possessions on the Gulf of Mexico, and not domineered over by any British possession whatever. In case of a war with Great Britain, our vessels bound to Chagres, would be obliged to sail almost within gunshot of the British forts at Jamaica. The Mississippi River being the great artery of the West, and the Mississippi Valley destined to be the great reservoir of the population, enterprise, and nationality of the United States, we are at all times better prepared to defend, the Isthmus of Tehuantepec than any other position on this side of our continent south of New Orleans.

In a late speech in Congress, advocating the North Pacific R. R., and taking the ground that the Union Pacific R. R. will be entirely inadequate to meet the demand of trade, and that in less than ten years, *three* distinct roads will be required, stretching entirely across the continent, of an aggregate length of over 9,000 miles, it is stated as a modern discovery, or, at all events, quoted as the opinions of the most intelligent living statesmen of Europe, "that the day is not far distant when the trade between the continent of Europe and Asia will be carried across this country."

This is, as we have seen, precisely the view entertained by Columbus himself, and all the marvelous developments in mechanical science during the last 400 years, tending to improvement in the art of navigation, have served but to confirm the accuracy of his judgment; and, it is not presumptuous in us to maintain, even in this day of great discovery, that whatever improvement may take place in the art of moving heavy burdens on land, the transport by water will always maintain its present advantage of superior economy ; and were there a strait through the Isthmus free to navigation, without delay or hindrance of any kind, who would say that the commerce of the world would seek a land carriage of over 3,000 miles, rather than an increase of ocean navigation of a few hundreds? Every argument then in favor of the construction of the Pacific R. R., based on the benefits thereby to be conferred on the commerce between Europe and Asia, has additional weight when urged in favor of the shorter land route over the Isthmus, and we propose so to make use of them.

It is true that no such passage exists, connecting the two oceans, nor can the art of man devise one. The very best that can be effected will be a ship canal with locks. If a passage shall be discovered which did not require a summit to be overcome by lockage (and which has repeatedly been claimed to have been discovered, and in consequence has given rise to great expectations), still the difference in level between the tides of the two oceans of some twenty-one feet, would render locks necessary ; but the passage said to have been recently explored by De Lacharme, with a summit of but 178 feet above tide, debouches into San Miguel Bay on the Pacific, and beyond the line within which the State of Granada have by the terms of their grant to the Panama R. R. Co. restricted themselves in the event of any future grant for the construction of a canal between the oceans. Hence the Cushing grant, so called, cannot avail of this wonderful discovery, or if so, it would appear to be in conflict with the grant to the Panama R. R. ; but all collateral evidence disproves the existence of any such pass.* An American engineer of great experience who had resided in that country for many years, selected and surveyed what he reports as the most feasible line between the two oceans for a ship

* Since writing the above, we see that the N. Granada government have thus far failed to ratify the Cushing grant.

canal, and reports the expense as $325,000,000. (See report to Congress of Admiral Davis on Inter-oceanic Canals and Railroads in 1867.) In other words, if practicable, it will be at such an expenditure of time and money, that the present generation cannot hope to see the project realized. For all commercial purposes of the present we must then look to railroads across the Isthmus, rather than canals; and in confirmation of this, in the speech above referred to, a quotation is made from Lord Bury, as follows: "Our trade (English) on the Pacific Ocean with China and with India must ultimately be carried on through our North American possessions. At any rate our political and commercial supremacy will have utterly departed from us if we neglect that just and important consideration, and if we fail to carry out to its fullest extent the physical advantages which our country offers to us, and which we have only to stretch out our hand to take advantage of."

And that this continent is not considered as a barrier to a close connection between the East and West, the following paper read before the British North American Association, by Col Synge of the Royal Engineers, is also quoted. "America is geographically a connecting link between the continents of Europe and Asia, and not a monstrous barrier between them. It lays in the track of the nearest and best connection, and this fact needs only to be fully recognized to render it in practice what it unquestionably is in the essential points of distance and direction."

A great body of statistics is also quoted in this speech, showing the enormous increase of trade in later years, and finding a close relation between this increase and the development of the railroad system in these various countries, and claiming for the Pacific R. R., the great bulk of this increase in the carrying trade between Europe and Asia.

It is true that the above roads will accommodate and will create a large amount of travel and trade, but this will be owing in a great measure to the local traffic due to the great increase of population following the development of the vast mineral wealth of our growing territories and Western states, which no other line of transit across the country could supply; but to suppose that the heavy traffic between Europe and Asia, or even between our own Atlantic seaboard and Asia, will follow the land route rather than the ocean, is simply in opposition to well established principles of trade, notwithstanding the fact is admitted that *time* is a far more important element in commercial transactions than formerly; but we must bear in mind the axiom, "that commerce seeks the cheapest and shortest transit," and the nations that can supply these will control it.

The estimate of business for the Pacific Roads includes, as an important item, teas from China,* not one pound of which will ever take the Pacific Railroad on its way to Europe. Even supposing that the loss and damage occasioned by over 3,000 miles of incessant "pounding and shaking up" was not in itself a sufficient objection, which we are assured by experienced merchants is in fact the case.

The Pacific Railroad Company's Report of 1868, in estimating the income of that road, make two capital mistakes.

In the first place, they estimate all the trade and travel now taken by sea steamers and sailing vessels around the Cape, as taken on their road; and, in the second place, they estimate the receipts for transporting this freight at $1\frac{88}{100}$ cents per ton per mile. With reference to the first, we would observe, that supplies from the east to the mining regions of the west, or emigration to these regions, will of necessity take their road; business relations between the extremes of

---

* It is likewise shown (Parliam. papers, 1866, vol. 26) that the amount of teas imported into Great Britain alone in the three years of 1863, '64, and '65, was 382,319,173 lbs., or 191,159 tons.

the same country will avail of the saving of time effected by this road; but the emigration and the traffic growing out of it, for the whole western coast of America, north and south, the products of the industry and development of that region, the trade and commerce of Australia, Sandwich Islands, Japan, China, and the East Indies, will take the route by the Isthmus, as far cheaper, and better suited to the wants of that trade, as we propose to show.

In the second place, with reference to the charge for freight on the railroad, as will appear elsewhere, the estimate of $1\frac{88}{100}$ cents per ton per mile is but one-half of the charge for freight in the Eastern States, and, of course, wholly inadequate to the wants of the Pacific Railroad, which will be a road uncommonly expensive to operate and keep in repair; and it appears from the statement of General Meigs, appended to the same report, p. 32, that, in truth, the charge for freight is $190 instead of $34, or 10½ cents per ton per mile, which is confirmed by the statement in the body of the report, "that the present rates are four times the tariff of Eastern roads."

We quote pp. 29 and 30 of U. P. R. R. Report of 1868, and also from p. 19 of the Report of 1867. We must be understood, however, as by no means aiming to detract anything from the merits of this road as a public benefit of the highest order, but if we appropriate a peal or two of its thunder, it will scarcely be missed, and is more applicable to our case than to theirs.

From Report of 1868.

"We have some authentic facts on which to base a fair estimate of the business of the Pacific Railroad, when it is completed, derived from Shipping Lists, Insurance Companies, Railroads, and general information:

Ships going from the Atlantic round Cape Horn—100.	80,000 Tons.
Steamships connecting at Panama with California and China—55	120,000 "
Overland Trains, Stages, Horses, &c.	30,000 "

"Thus we have two hundred and thirty thousand tons carried westward; and experience has shown, that in the last few years, the returned passengers from California have been nearly as numerous as those going. So also the great mass of gold and silver flows eastward; latterly there is an importation of wheat from California and goods from China by the Pacific route. We may fairly assume, therefore, that the trade each way will be about equal; we have then 460,000 tons as *the actual freight across the continent.*

"How many passengers have we? We make the following estimate from the average of people:

110 (both ways) steamships................	50,000
200 " " vessels....................	4,000
Overland (both ways)....................	100,000
Number per annum..................	154,000

"At present prices (averaging half the cost of the steamships), for both passengers and tonnage, we have this result:

154,000 passengers at $100.............	$15,400,000
460,000 tons rated at $1 per cubic foot....	15,640,000
Present Cost of Transportation......	$31,040,000

"There can be no doubt that the number of passengers will be more than doubled by the completion of the road; so also, the road would take all the very light and valuable goods, which would be greatly increased *by the China trade.* Taking these things into view—estimating passengers at 7½ cents per mile, and goods at $1 per cubic foot—we have

300,000 passengers at $150 each.........	$45,000,000
300,000 tons at $34 (per cubic foot)......	10,200,000
Gross receipts........................	$55,200,000

"Suppose that the portion accruing to the Union Pacific is $30,000,000, estimate the running expenses at one-half, and this would leave a net profit of $15,000,000.

" This may seem very large to those who have not examined the subject, but it must be remembered—1st, that the longest lines of road are the most profitable; 2d, that this road connects two oceans, and the vast populations of Western Europe and Eastern Asia; 3d, that the immense mining regions of Idaho, Montana, Nevada, California, just developing, will produce a transit of persons and freight at present beyond belief. We leave this estimate on record as a moderate (not an exaggerated) view of the business and profits which may be fairly expected from the Grand Pacific Railroad."

" Estimates of *future* business are doubtless valuable and important, and it does not follow that they are always too large. When the New York & Erie Railroad was first projected, its future business was estimated by its friends at *three* millions per annum, while it is now *over fifteen* millions, and will steadily increase. It must be remembered that for many years to come this Union Pacific and its western connections will be the *only* Pacific Railroad, and, as it will be without competition, *it can always charge remunerative prices.* While the present rates are four times the tariff of eastern roads, they are not one-fourth of of the former cost by teams, of which twenty-seven thousand left two points on the Missouri River on their westward journey, within a single year."

" The anticipation of the early completion of the Pacific Railroad has recently stimulated all kinds of productive industry in California to prepare for that means of rapid communication which is so soon to multiply her numbers and wealth in a greater ratio than ever. Factories are being erected, large flouring mills established, vineyards planted, and farms extended, that the State may be ready to receive the great tide of population that must soon flow into it over the track of the Pacific Railroad. The East is also preparing to accommodate itself to the forthcoming changes in the current of business. The Pacific Mail Steamship Company of New York is now running a regular line of its splendid steamers between San Francisco and China and Japan, which is doubtless the pioneer of other lines, that will traverse the Pacific Ocean laden with the teas, spices, and other products of Eastern Asia. Excepting some very heavy or bulky articles, of comparatively low values, shortness of time decides the direction of freights, and most of these cargoes will find their natural transit over the Union Pacific Railroad."

The dogma, "that the longest roads are the most profitable," only hold true so far as their increased length furnishes additional way traffic. A thousand miles of road over a desert cannot be run so cheaply per mile as one of a hundred miles! The proof of this requires no argument. The hint, "that the road will for a long time to come be without competition," is something which we can safely count on. The assertion that, "shortness of time decides the direction of freight," is only true to a certain extent; the reduction of fifty per cent. or more on the freight charges will inevitably determine its direction almost irrespective of time.

It would be in error to assume the present rates of freight on existing lines as a standard by which to compare the absolute cost of new lines of traffic. We may state as an illustration of the truth of this, and in evidence of the value of a little wholesome competition, that the rates established by the Panama R. R. Company have enabled them to pay dividends equal to the entire cost of the construction of their very expensive road, within four years of its being opened for travel, and a large trade still doubles Cape Horn for the western coast of South and Central America, which a more judicious policy would have secured to this road. This large and increasing commerce (of the western coast of South and Central America) is, however, still a monopoly to the railroad, the value of which we have no means of judging, no published returns being made. We only know, that judging of the future by the past, the only hope for that magnificent region of Central and South America lies in opening a competing route for its trade, and thus aid in stimulating branches of industry which only lies dormant for lack of encouragement. The excessive charges of this railroad have hampered and retarded, not only the trade of that coast, but the development of all connecting lines of sea steamers, which have been compelled to render the lion's share of profit to less than fifty miles of land transit. The prices current of freight of the Pacific Mail Steamship Company show their charges from New York to Aspinwall, a distance of 2,400 miles, at 25 cents per cubic foot, whilst the charge on the railroad alone is from 25c. to 75c. per foot for freight and $25 for every passenger. What is called "slow freight" from New York to San Francisco by the Pacific Mail Steamship Company is charged at $60 (gold) a ton measurement, whilst the "fast freight" is charged at $140 the ton (gold). The speed of the steamers is in each case the same, but the difference of time of ten days between the fast and slow freight occurs at the Isthmus of Panama, where the railroad company benefits largely by the despatch. In 1863, a cargo of tea was taken from China to London by screw steamer, a distance of 17,000 miles in 80 days, at a freight of $60 a ton. The distance by steamer and by the Isthmus from San Francisco to New York being 6,218 miles, for which $140 is charged, the time being 25 days.

It will be seen from these examples that we are driven, in determining the cost of freighting, to disregard the freight charges on the various lines, and assume a fair paying price based upon collateral evidence of the value of the service.

The estimate which we propose to give of the cost

of transport by the various lines does not therefore pretend to extreme accuracy. A fair paying rate for freighting, exclusive of insurance or other charges is all we can offer. It will, however, be *comparatively* correct, the other charges incidental to shifting freight, insurance, &c., will differ so little on the various routes, as not to affect materially the comparisons of *relative* cost.

The charge for freight, as now established on the Pacific Road, taken from the published reports, is 10½ cts. per ton (34 feet measurement) per mile, from Omaha West. The Railroad returns for the last year of the movement of freight on the established roads at the East is nearly 4 cts. per ton per mile. We will say 3 cts. The running time for freight is never over 12 miles an hour. On the Pacific Road it can never net, for a through freight fare, over 10 miles an hour including stoppages. The speed of sea steamers is taken from the average of the log-books of the steamers running on the Panama line both ways in the Pacific and Atlantic Oceans.

FREIGHTS FOR HOME TRADE.

		AMOUNT.	TIME DAYS.
From New York to San Francisco via Pacific Railroad, 3,361 miles, as follows:			
From New York to Omaha, at 3c. per mile..	$43 95		
" Omaha to San Francisco, 10½c. "	199 00		
	$242 95=gold	$179 25	14
For general merchandise, per ton of 34 feet cube..			
From New York to Aspinwall........	2,392 miles.		
" Aspinwall to Panama..........	51		
" Panama to San Francisco	3,775		
	6,218 miles.		
For general merchandise, per ton of 40 feet cube..		$140	22 to 25

FREIGHTS FOR EUROPEAN TRADE.

	AMOUNT.	TIME DAYS.
From England (Liverpool) to New York, 3,000 miles, general merchandise per ton measurement....	5 50	10
From New York to San Francisco, 3,361 miles, by Union Pacific Railroad, present price........	179 25	14
From San Francisco to Hong Kong, 6,470 miles...	20 00	30
Total from Liverpool to Hong Kong via Pacific Railroad.................	$204 75	54
From England (Southampton) for general merchandise, per ton of 40 feet measurement, to Hong Kong via Panama and San Francisco (see tariff of the Royal Mail Steamship Packet Company).................. .£19 15s. =	$98 75	60
From France*(Havre) to New York, per ton measurement..................................	5 00	10
From New York to San Francisco via Pacific Railroad.......	179 25	14
From San Francisco to Hong Kong	20 00	30
Total from Havre to Hong Kong via Pacific Railroad	$204 25	54
From France (Saint Nazaire) to Hong Kong for general merchandise, per ton of 40 feet, via Panama and San Francisco (see tariff of the Compagnie Generale Transatlantique, published in February, 1869) ;............F. 525 =	$105 00	60
From England (Liverpool) to Aspinwall, 4,782 miles..................................	35 20	18
From Aspinwall to Panama, 51 miles............	20 00	1
From Panama in direct line to Hong Kong, 9,567 miles, price estimated from Pacific Mail Steamship Co.'s present rates, charged via San Francisco..................................	37 00	35
Total from Liverpool in direct line to Hong Kong via Panama............................	$92 20	54
From France (Saint Nazaire) to Hong Kong in direct line from Panama (including the estimated price from there to Hong Kong from Pacific Mail Steamship Co.'s present rates)...	$92 00	54

The following tariff table of the Compagnie Generale Transatlantique (published on the 15th February last), shows the freights to Europe on productions of Japan and China, particularly on tea, transported with the above-named speed :

Merchandise.	Tonnage.	From Yokohama, Nagasaki, Shanghai, and Hong Kong, to		
		Saint Nazaire.	Paris, Lyons, Marseilles, and Havre.	London.
Silk	40 feet cube, or ton weight............	$120	$128	$130
Tea	40 feet cube	69	77	79
General merchandise.	40 feet cube, or 2,240 pounds	95	103	105

I think it will be conceded, from the above statement, that neither for the European trade, nor for the trade from our Atlantic ports, will the Pacific Railroad offer any advantage over the route by the way of the Isthmus. I omit all mention of fast passenger travel.

We have made the comparison thus far with the Isthmus route via Panama, from the fact that the present steamship lines both on the Atlantic and Pacific, whose times and rates are known, run in connection with that road, and estimates of freighting based on these rates cannot be questioned.

If, then, the advantages of trade and commerce between the continents are in favor of this Isthmus, what must be the advantages accruing to the route by way of the Isthmus of Tehuantepec, which lies some 1,200 miles farther north than that of Panama?

The following distances, being the log reckonings of steamships, are taken from T. I. Cram's Topographical Engineers U. S. A. Report on Ocean Routes, published in 1857:

	MILES.
From New York to Aspinwall	2,393
" " Minatitlan	2,275
" Panama to San Francisco	3,775
" Tehuantepec "	2,304
" New York to San Francisco via Panama	6,218
" " " via Tehuantepec	4,741
Difference from New York in favor of the Tehuantepec route	1,477

This difference appears still greater for the commerce of the Southern ports of the United States, say New Orleans:

	MILES.
From New Orleans to San Francisco via Panama	5,718
" " " via Tehuantepec	3,384
Difference from New Orleans in favor of the Tehuantepec route.	2,334

At the present speed of the steamers on the Panama route, allowing for one day to cross the Isthmus at either point, the saving of time from New York to San Francisco, by taking the Tehuantepec route rather than the Panama, is six days. From New Orleans to San Francisco, by the Tehuantepec route, there is a saving of nine days.

Need the comparison be extended any further? From Otis's Hand-book of the Panama Road, p. 52, we learn: "In 1858 the business over the road from the western coast of South and Central America exceeded in value *nine* times the freighting business of California via the Isthmus; and in 1860 fourteen-fifteenths of the entire freighting business of the road was from shipments from the United States and England, and the return products of South and Central America, such as indigo, cochineal, india-rubber, coffee, deerskins and goatskins, dye woods, pearl shells, tobacco, balsams, Peruvian bark, ores, straw hats," &c. When the inconceivable richness of these regions is taken into consideration, coupled with the fact that the transport across the Isthmus by the Panama Road is not cheapened, but the establishment of lines of steamers alone has developed the existing trade, we can judge what would be the effect of opening a rival line, which, itself passing through a country of unexampled productiveness, and with a safe port on the western coast easy of access (neither of which is the case at Panama) shall, instead of charging $30 a ton for carrying manufactured tobacco (and a like rate for other native products) a distance of 46 miles, charge but half that amount for a land transport of 162 miles! We say that, instead of presenting a long array of figures of statistics of the native trade, we need but point to what the Panama Railroad has reaped already from this trade, and claim at least an equal return.

www.ingramcontent.com/pod-product-compliance
Lightning Source LLC
LaVergne TN
LVHW011218110826
845150LV00006B/1463

9781425517021